THE LITTLE BOOK OF Restorative Justice & Community

THE LITTLE BOOKS OF JUSTICE & PEACEBUILDING

Published titles include:

The Little Book of Restorative Justice: Revised & Updated, by Howard Zehr

The Little Book of Conflict Transformation, by John Paul Lederach

The Little Book of Family Group Conferences, New-Zealand Style, by Allan MacRae and Howard Zehr

The Little Book of Strategic Peacebuilding, by Lisa Schirch

The Little Book of Strategic Negotiation, by Jayne Seminare Docherty

The Little Book of Circle Processes, by Kay Pranis

The Little Book of Contemplative Photography, by Howard Zehr

Little Book of Healthy Organizations, by David Brubaker and Ruth Hoover Zimmerman

The Little Book of Restorative Discipline for Schools, by Lorraine Stutzman Amstutz and Judy H. Mullet

The Little Book of Trauma Healing, by Carolyn Yoder

The Little Book of Biblical Justice, by Chris Marshall

The Little Book of Restorative Justice for People in Prison, by Barb Toews

The Little Book of Cool Tools for Hot Topics, by Ron Kraybill and Evelyn Wright

El Pequeño Libro de Justicia Restaurativa, by Howard Zehr

The Little Book of Dialogue for Difficult Subjects, by Lisa Schirch and David Campt

The Little Book of Victim Offender Conferencing, by Lorraine Stutzman Amstutz

The Little Book of Restorative Justice for Colleges and Universities, by David R. Karp

The Little Book of Restorative Justice for Sexual Abuse, by Judah Oudshoorn with Michelle Jackett and Lorraine Stutzman Amstutz

The Big Book of Restorative Justice: Four Classic Justice & Peacebuilding Books in One Volume, by Howard Zehr, Lorraine Stutzman Amstutz, Allan MacRae, and Kay Pranis

The Little Book of Transformative Community Conferencing, by David Anderson Hooker

The Little Book of Restorative Justice in Education, by Katherine Evans and Dorothy Vaandering

The Little Book of Restorative Justice for Older Adults, by Julie Friesen and Wendy Meek

The Little Book of Race and Restorative Justice, by Fania E. Davis

The Little Book of Racial Healing, by Thomas Norman DeWolf, Jodie Geddes

The Little Book of Restorative Teaching Tools, by Lindsey Pointer, Kathleen McGoey, and Haley Farrar

Little Book of Restorative Teaching Tools for Online Learning, by Kathleen McGoey and Lindsey Pointer

The Little Book of Police Youth Dialogue, by Dr. Micah E. Johnson and Jeffrey Weisberg

The Little Book of Youth Engagement in Restorative Justice, by Evelín Aquino, Heather Bligh Manchester, and Anita Wadhwa

The Little Book of Restorative Justice Program Design, by Alisa Del Tufo and E. Quin Gonell

Little Book of Listening, by Sharon Browning, Donna Duffey, Fred Magondu, John A. Moore, and Patricia A. Way

Little Book of Restorative Justice for Campus Sexual Harms, by Rachel Roth Sawatzky and Mikayla W-C McCray

Little Book of Environment and Restorative Justice, by Wanbli Wapháha Hokšíla, Nirson Medeiros da Silva Neto, João Salm, Josineide Gadelha Pamplona Medeiros

The Little Books of Justice & Peacebuilding present, in highly accessible form, key concepts and practices from the fields of restorative justice, conflict transformation, and peacebuilding. Written by leaders in these fields, they are designed for practitioners, students, and anyone interested in justice, peace, and conflict resolution.

The Little Books of Justice & Peacebuilding series is a cooperative effort between the Center for Justice and Peacebuilding of Eastern Mennonite University and publisher Good Books.

THE LITTLE BOOK OF Restorative Justice & Community

Reclaiming Connection and Responsibility for Our Neighbors

SHERYL WILSON
AND CAITLIN MORNEAU

Good Books
New York, New York

Good Books books may be purchased in bulk at special discounts for sales promotion, corporate gifts, fund-raising, or educational purposes. Special editions can also be created to specifications. For details, contact the Special Sales Department, Good Books, 307 Fifth Avenue, 4th Floor, New York, NY 10016 or info@skyhorsepublishing.com.

Good Books is an imprint of Skyhorse Publishing, Inc.®, a Delaware corporation.

Visit our website at www.goodbooks.com.

10 9 8 7 6 5 4 3 2 1

Library of Congress Cataloging-in-Publication Data is available on file.

Cover design by Kai Texel
Cover photo by Howard Zehr
Series editor: Barb Toews

Print ISBN: 978-1-68099-952-5
Ebook ISBN: 978-1-68099-957-0

Printed in the United States of America

Contents

Chapter 1: Introduction 1

Chapter 2: What Is Community? 11

Chapter 3: Barriers to Community 19

Chapter 4: Restorative Justice 28

Chapter 5: Responding When Harm Occurs in Community 45

Chapter 6: Restorative Community 62

Chapter 7: Roles to Build Restorative Communities 79

Chapter 8: Restorative Self 88

Chapter 9: Realizing Beloved Community 102

Recommended Resources 108

Endnotes 110

Chapter 1
Introduction

Love is creative and redemptive. Love builds up and unites; hate tears down and destroys. The aftermath of the "fight with fire" method which you suggest is bitterness and chaos, the aftermath of the love method is reconciliation and creation of the beloved community.

—Martin Luther King Jr.[1]

Dr. Martin Luther King Jr. offers the ultimate vision of community, where all of humankind is in right relationship with one another. However, for many of us, this vision feels desperately out of reach. Whether we are personally impacted by violence, broadly concerned about oppression and injustice, or simply feeling hurt and isolated, genuine connection with others may feel distant or elusive. Simultaneously, many of us can recall moments when mutual care and respect prevailed in a group—moments of comfort, celebration, and yes, even suffering. These are places and spaces where each person is honored and cherished in their wholeness (brokenness included), where goodwill resonates, even amid diversity of thought, experience, and background.

These occasions offer us glimpses of the beloved community, which Dr. King described as a "society where caring and compassion drive political policies that support the worldwide elimination of poverty and hunger and all forms of bigotry and violence. At its core, the 'Beloved Community' is an engine of reconciliation."[2] The idea of a beloved community is also demonstrated in the African concept of *ubuntu*, roughly meaning "I am because we are."[3] In Zulu tradition, this philosophy acknowledges "the humanity of man,"[4] and in Bantu it roughly translates as "humanity."

Dr. King started speaking about the concept of a beloved community after the Montgomery bus boycott of the 1950s. This idea continued to surface in other speeches throughout his life. Dr. King wasn't just sharing lofty ideas when he discussed the beloved community. He really believed that such a community is achievable when everyone feels valued, all members have a voice, people have a sense of belonging, and oppression is no more. Today, the idea of a beloved community paints a picture of what it means to be our best selves, as individuals and in relationship with one another, in various groups.

Years ago, I lived in a tight-knit city block. We looked out for each other and were proud of being multigenerational, multiethnic, and diverse. One day, a friend called me about a news story: a teenage girl had hidden her pregnancy, placed her newborn in the garbage, and left the child for dead. The baby was miraculously found alive. I insisted it couldn't be anyone from my neighborhood—I knew my neighbors too well. But later I learned the baby's father was my neighbor's grandson, and the couple had been living there quietly.

For a while, I wrestled with thoughts of what to do. Unfortunately, I gave in to the voices of "minding my own business" and did nothing.

How could I have been a better neighbor? I ask myself that now all the time.

—Sheryl

Community and Restorative Justice

Restorative justice offers a pathway to realizing these visions of community because the practices and principles offer a reconciling response to harm as well as a framework for nurturing trust, connection, and resilience in ways that also help to prevent harm in the first place. Often the three parties named in a restorative process are "victim," "offender," and "community." Considerable attention is rightly dedicated to centering and amplifying the needs and obligations of people most directly impacted by or involved in the harm at hand.

Though frequently named, less attention is focused on the experiences or roles of community members who are witnesses of the harm, adjacent to it, or indirectly impacted by it. The result is that "community" is loosely defined. This ambiguity allows for flexibility and creativity, but can also lead to confusion and disengagement. Community members may rightly ask themselves questions like: What is my role in this situation? How do I understand my own reactions and feelings within the bigger story of what is happening? Have I done my best to support possibilities for justice and healing? Often, it is hard to "know your lane." Between "minding one's business" and being "in someone's business" is the business of being a good neighbor and playing a role in preventing and repairing harm. Whether one is a family member, friend, neighbor, concerned citizen, or system actor, the range of needs, obligations, and opportunities to engage with restorative justice processes are vast.

This book aims to explore restorative justice and community as a nested model that includes multiple levels of relationships—individual, interpersonal, communal, and societal. Each level represents different restorative work:

- **Individual** explores one's interior life through *inner work*, personal reflection, and consideration of one's personal gifts and areas for growth;
- **Interpersonal** is concerned with *restorative responses to harm*, including identifying harm and the person(s) impacted and opportunities or desires for repair and engaging with restorative responses in various ways to support people directly impacted by harm;
- **Communal** focuses on *restorative communities*, through which the groups and affiliations within which we operate, including those that are institutional or organizational, commit to an ethic of restorative justice;
- **Societal** represents the *beloved community*, the destination toward which individual, interpersonal, and communal restorative justice build.

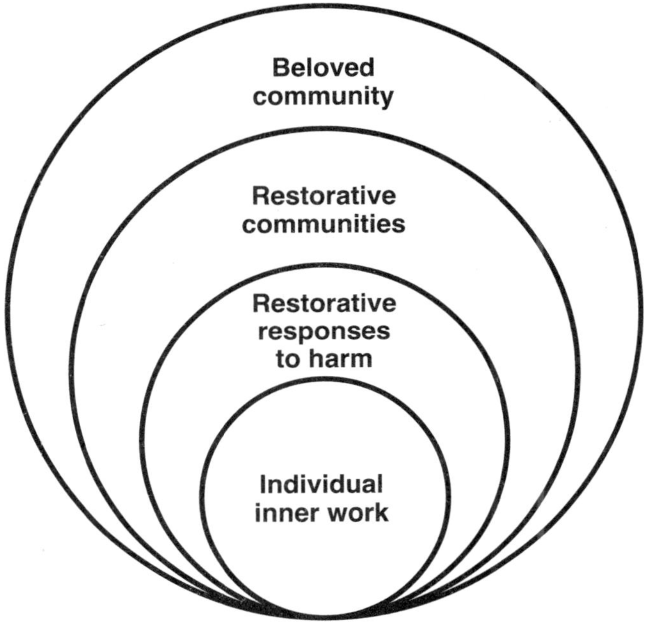

In this exploration, we will aim to add clarity to questions like:

- What is community?
- What are barriers to community that restorative justice may overcome?
- What are the signposts of a community that is on a journey to become more restorative?
- What are the roles and responsibilities of community members in responding to harm restoratively and building restorative community?

> While walking with my family one day, neighbors relayed that a young man had been fatally shot at the apartment complex just around the corner. A bystander restrained the shooter until police arrived. Then, when returning to our house, I watched as my middle-aged neighbor was met by a group of young people who embraced her as she screamed. My neighbor's firstborn son, father of her two-year-old grandchild, had been killed.
>
> Part of me wanted to rush over. Another voice inside me said, "It's not your place." She was with loved ones. I had my small children in tow—there was no way for me to be helpful in that moment. But as I returned home, moved through dinner and bedtime, and eventually lay in bed, I wondered and prayed: *What is mine to do?*
>
> —Caitlin

Who Is This Little Book for?

This book is for people who want to discern when to show up and how to be as supportive as possible to fellow community members, especially when harm occurs. And it is for those who want to develop a greater sense of belonging within their communities and among their constituent groups. This book is also for restorative justice practitioners, as it may complement their existing approaches to community member participation and create a springboard for further exploration of this topic. Finally, for supporters of restorative practices, we hope that the learnings shared here may ignite fresh ideas for community engagement.

Who We Are as Authors

We both have backgrounds in restorative justice practices, including facilitating restorative dialogues and supporting families whose loved ones died by homicide. As such, we are each attuned to the personal suffering, the violated relationships, and the emotional, spiritual, and material needs that play out within our communities and among loved ones. We each encounter the internal and external cultural voices that advise us to "keep your distance" or "mind your business" and have asked questions of ways that community can respond to and prevent crime that go beyond the theoretical, or even professional. These questions are very personal, as our earlier stories suggest.

Sheryl

I began my journey of understanding restorative justice as a student taking a class in mediation and conflict resolution. It was there, in Mark Umbreit's class at the University of Minnesota, that I first heard the words "restorative" and "justice" used together. Restorative justice was poetic and meaningful, and it was illuminating to find out about a type of justice I had never heard of, but absolutely needed to understand. It made sense to this southern, Black, post-Civil Rights-era-beneficiary history buff. At the end of the seminar, I felt called to make this my career path.

Since that time, I have found ways to repair harm in my own life and further study restorative justice. I went on to write a master's thesis on how the civil rights movement provided a blueprint for the restorative justice movement. I deepened my understanding of historical harm and how restorative justice can address its impact and create paths for repair.

As I grew more knowledgeable about the ways that harm occurs, it became clearer to me how to support those who have been harmed and those who cause harm. It has been more challenging, however, to figure out how to support the role of the bystanders, witnesses, and those peripheral to harm. I wondered how to hold accountable those who are in the role of community.

Caitlin

Community life was essentially my foundation for understanding restorative justice. Well before formal study or practice, I lived and worked in intentional Christian communities that held relationships as paramount. In times of conflict or when harm occurred, rather than sweeping it under the rug or kicking people out, these communities embraced repair and reintegration through dialogue, actualizing the synergies of mercy and responsibility. When attending to local social inequity, these communities held in balance lofty visions and current realities, common good and individual dignity, structure and flexibility, impactful change and simple presence—invaluable lessons, for me, in the labor of movement building.

Having grown up in the Catholic Archdiocese of Boston during the first major public allegations of the clergy sexual abuse, I was sensitive at an early age to the pain of victims and the community devastation that occurs when trust, connection, and institutional accountability erode. In retrospect, I can see how these experiences laid the foundation for my orientation to the principles and practices of restorative justice and my commitment to advancing them within the faith community that I call home.

Now, accompanying faith leaders who seek to transform the US criminal legal system, I arrive as a fellow community member. In doing so, my own experiences of harm, both suffered and caused, invite me to humbly identify with my brothers and sisters who are directly impacted by crime and incarceration. These convictions compel me to seek out people and groups, in whose company I may become a better version of myself, a contributor to the well-being of others, and an agent of healing, peace, and reconciliation.

About This Book

A global reality of a beloved community is likely unattainable in our lifetimes. However, the quality of relationship that it evokes is absolutely within reach, and the principles and practices of restorative justice help pave a pathway for realizing this in big and small ways. This book offers a start on that path. You may already have a particular community in mind. As you read further, you may also view your various communities with fresh eyes.

The next two chapters will discuss the various ways we define community and what issues cause barriers to community. Chapter 4 explores restorative justice philosophy and practice, including how it can take shape in community life. Chapter 5 offers ways in which community members can respond when harm occurs. Chapters 6 and 7 propose a framework of twelve principles for "restorative community" and introduce roles for community members to help create such a community. Chapter 8 invites readers to consider their inner life as a way to cultivate a "restorative self," and to discern the various roles we may hold as community members. We close the book in Chapter 9 with encouragement to put the book's lessons into practice. When offering examples of and reference points for the book's themes, we point to various types of harm-doing, including crime and hurts that happen in day-to-day life, and offer stories of community that apply material in real ways.

As we write this book, the political and societal landscape of the United States is in a state of upheaval. Communities as we know them (or thought we knew them) are being both dismantled and forged. Regardless of when you are reading this book, you may be searching for, or in a state of disillusionment with, your own notions of community. In these times when society tells us to "look the other way" if we are not directly involved with a harmful event, this book can provide an alternative and focused path for us as community members.

No matter your entry point to restorative justice, or this text, we hope you will come away sensing that beloved community is for all of us and become inspired to embrace restorative justice to build toward that vision.

Chapter 2
What Is Community?

When we intentionally create a community for the purpose of a shared goal, it can deepen relationships, create feelings of belonging, and provide support for the health and wellbeing of all members. Community is a gateway to better understand our own lives and the lives of others and creates an essential foundation for people working toward common goals.

—National Museum of African American History and Culture[1]

What comes to mind when you hear the word "community"? Jot down the first three to five words that surface for you. If you asked this question to a room full of people, you would likely compile a list of words like *friends, family, neighborhood, school, workplace, faith group,* or *city.* Whether we formally sign up to be part of a club, live in proximity to others, or realize an affiliation over time, we are all part of different types of communities. This chapter lays the groundwork for understanding restorative justice and community by discussing these and other common understandings of community and the ways community influences us and our perspectives on responses to harm.

Common Communities

The Oxford English Dictionary defines community as "a group of people living in the same place or having a particular characteristic in common." As we consider the different common characteristics that make up "community," remember that there are many ways in which communities have the potential to overlap with each other. Additionally, someone may share a characteristic with others but not feel a sense of community with them.

Culture

Community may be formed through a common heritage or culture. These connections can come from biological or ancestral lineage, passed down through family relations, ethnic background, and language. Membership spans generations and brings to mind ancestors who have passed, elders, children, and future descendants. It is important to remember, however, that culture is not only a part of one's identity and that it is dynamic and ever changing, not static.

Experience

Community may be forged through common experiences, especially ones that are challenging. People who have lost loved ones to violence often say that murder "changed their address book." People who have been displaced by war or natural disaster, though coming from very different parts of the world, may relate because of the hardship through which they have lived. Other common experiences might be related to education, housing status, marital or parenting circumstances, community service, or charitable or advocacy commitments.

Location and Land

Community may stem from connections to a physical region—such as a town, city, or neighborhood—in which a person resides. These communities might include Indigenous peoples, residents, business owners, educators, civil servants, and lawmakers. For some, the way they locate themselves within a community does not require residency. For example, a person may move to a new city but maintain a sense of connection and pride with the region where they were raised.

Others' communities may be with a particular geography or the land. Indigenous peoples may feel connection with ancestors who inhabited the land prior to settler colonization, land theft, and cultural erasure. Non-Indigenous individuals may also experience a sense of community with Indigenous communities through their solidarity with Indigenous struggles to be seen and heard. All of us may feel connected to the land due to recent experiences or memories. This type of community goes beyond present-day boundary lines and jurisdictions and may span many generations.

> I was born in Tallahassee, Florida, a place that is reminiscent of the deep south, as it borders Alabama and Georgia and is the home of Florida A & M University, an historically Black institution. I grew up seeing a thriving Black community

> where I had role models who looked like me and demonstrated varying forms of Black excellence: we lived in close proximity to college professors, coaches, city officials, and community organizers. I grew up with high aspirations of what I wanted to be when I grew up. I am so grateful for that.
>
> —Sheryl

Interests

Commitment to a shared area of interest often leads to a sense of community, even with people we have never met. These affiliations can be especially broad, from hobbies, to professions, to sports teams, to areas of study and many more. Affiliation with such communities may take the form of regular gatherings, bumper stickers, social media groups and posts, and even graphic T-shirts.

Beliefs

Community may grow around common religious, spiritual, philosophical, or ideological beliefs. Though less visible, they nevertheless shape our moral perspectives and interpretations about how people, relationships, and the world operates. These may be recognizable through outward representations (clothing, yard signs, public statements) or ways of convening (worship services, public demonstrations), but are more often demonstrated through thoughts, words, and actions.

Humanity

With a shared humanity, community is not limited to a common location or characteristics, but is rather a oneness of all things and a belief in an infinite web of interdependence where diversity is appreciated and all are valued, flourishing, and safe. It is the idea of belonging to one human family. This community may be rooted, for instance, in a belief that a divine Creator gave all things life or in various cultural, spiritual, and ancestral understandings of interconnectedness.

Community Lessons

Whether we realize it or not, our communities teach us how to act and to be in relationship with one another. Two key lessons we learn from community are about norms and belonging, each of which shapes how we, as individuals or a community, respond when harm occurs.

Norms

Communities often set behavioral norms about what is considered acceptable or not and instruct us how to, for instance, speak, dress, eat, move, spend time, handle money, and treat the environment. Each community will have their own standards or expectations for participation—such as what being an active member looks like, who leads or speaks for the group, or what experiences or skills are necessary.

Communities also set relational norms about how to treat and behave toward others, be they fellow members and peers, authority figures, or outsiders. It goes without saying that not all norms are healthy. For example, toxicity arises when there is a mismatch between what one says and what one does, like when an organizational leader says they have an open-door policy, but employees who voice a concern are shamed or retaliated against.

These norms instruct how members are expected to deal with conflict and harm. We all can probably think of times that as individuals or communities we have attempted to ignore a harm, hoping that it will go away or work itself out without intervention. It is not uncommon for members of a group to blame other members in determining or denying their own fault. There may also be times that a purposeful choice is made to disengage or create distance from the harm and those involved, in order not to escalate it further. A community may choose to manage the harm through set rules, policies, and procedures that guide how to identify rule violations and subsequent consequences. In some cases, a community may outsource harm management to an outside professional, the court system, or a third party. What's more, harm or conflict may further escalate when community subgroups disagree about how the original harm should be handled.

When harm occurs in a community, people tend to reevaluate their norms. For example, in the aftermath of a robbery, someone might install a security system or be more cautious with new people who are nearby. Maybe they wonder, alone or with others, what went wrong, if the harm could have been prevented in some way, or what things could have been different.

Belonging

People may know they belong because of a formal sign-up, affiliated symbolism, or attending an event. We may sense our belonging by the nature of welcome, familiarity, or ease in the presence of others. We may also make assumptions—knowingly or unknowingly, rightly or wrongly—about another person's communities based on dress, speech, or relationships.

When individuals experience a sense of belonging, they receive support, connection, and understanding and acceptance (especially cultural) from and by others within the community. It may lead to new relationships, such as a neighbor getting involved in the community garden, a student playing a sport at their school, or a church member joining the choir. This belonging then contributes to community meaning and purpose.

Experiences with conflict or harm may have a direct impact on one's sense of belonging. The person(s) directly harmed may find a new sense of belonging with others who have had similar experiences. For example, a mother whose child was murdered may find new connections with others who have lost a loved one to violence. At the same time, they may find it difficult to stay connected with preexisting communities, because their community cannot relate. The person who is responsible for harm may be removed from the community, either formally (fired) or socially ("canceled"). Those who are indirectly affected may choose to disaffiliate from the group either formally (quit) or socially (go silent).

Conclusion

No community is a monolith and there are a range of stories, experiences, and characteristics present within each. There are also many different ways that a person might define or describe their level of connection with the community itself, with not all experiences healthy or positive. Indeed, creating community can be challenging. Barriers to community can make it especially difficult to respond in healthy ways when faced with difference, conflict, and harm. In the next chapter, we explore some of these barriers.

Chapter 3
Barriers to Community

Beloved community is formed not by the eradication of difference but by its affirmation, by each of us claiming the identities and cultural legacies that shape who we are and how we live in the world.

—bell hooks[1]

Experience with community can be both beautiful and challenging. This chapter explores the ways in which we identify barriers that disconnect and divide people from each other. These barriers exist at the interpersonal level in how we struggle to listen, empathize, and tolerate difference. There are also structural barriers to community that manifest at historical, institutional, and systemic levels which, if not addressed, can lead to community complicity. When we understand these barriers and when they are operating in our relationships, we can more meaningfully take steps to reduce them. As you read, reflect on how these barriers may play out in your interpersonal and community relationships.

Interpersonal Barriers

Harm or conflict often emerges first within our interpersonal relationships and daily interactions with individuals with whom we live, work, socialize, or encounter. Sometimes harm takes us by surprise because we feel comfortable with someone and then find out they do not share our views, or they may not react sympathetically toward us. Other times, we are guarded when we enter a room, call, or event, anticipating friction, disagreement, or unwelcome. These experiences are natural in human relationships, yet we often act in ways that escalate or exacerbate such challenges and create barriers to community. Three such interpersonal barriers are the struggle to listen, inability to be empathetic, and intolerance to difference. Taken together, these three interpersonal barriers can lead to separation and othering, blame and finger pointing in the face of harm and conflict, and avoidance of our own responsibility for participation in a problem. It may contribute to urges to fix, solve, or fuel another person's pain.

Struggle to Listen

Listening is essential to building connection and understanding. However, we are often more occupied with what we want or plan to say or only pay partial attention, are distracted by devices or mental lists, or listen only enough to craft our response. When we reply, we may be quick to offer unsolicited advice, a counter argument, or personal opinion, without much regard for what the other person has actually said. We may change the subject or invalidate someone's feelings or reality of what they experienced, feeling uncomfortable or unsure of what to do. We may even leave the listening to trained professionals, thinking we have nothing to offer. With these reactions, we are not actually listening to understand, to be curious. By not truly listening, we miss what we need to hear from others, avoid the situation and the person, and thus lose the opportunity to be in relationship.

Withhold Empathy

The struggle to listen means we miss out on the opportunity to be empathetic. Brené Brown describes empathy as "feeling with people." She goes on to say, "It's simply listening, holding space, withholding judgment, emotionally connecting, and communicating that incredibly healing message of 'you're not alone.'"[2] Choosing empathy does not require you to agree with someone or support their behaviors, especially if they are causing harm to others, but it does invite a recognition of the stories and needs that are beneath the surface of their words or behaviors. When we neglect to practice empathy, we default instead to incomplete or erroneous assumptions about another person's experience and perspective. These assumptions (whether conscientious or not) run the risk of devaluing another person's humanity, making it all too easy to inflict and legitimize harm toward others.

Intolerance for Difference

The inability to listen and practice empathy can lead to an intolerance for difference. This mindset insists that if there is a problem, my viewpoint is right, yours is wrong, and we need to duke it out until one side wins and the other loses. This is closely linked with our tendency toward individualism and beliefs that we can survive on our own, do not need others for our well-being, and disregard concern for the well-being of others. This mindset plays out in subtle ways, such as our inability to genuinely listen to one another. In the extreme, it equates difference with threat, where those who think differently than us are seen as evil, less than human, and unworthy of care. It separates and silences people and enables subtle and overt violence toward others, which violates everyone's dignity. Cancel culture, when we shun, humiliate, or publicly shame someone for their beliefs and actions, is just one common example of an intolerance for difference.

> "Stand in the middle, 'cause that's where healing happens. That's where conversation happens. That's where change happens."
>
> —Tyler Perry[3]

Structural Barriers

Barriers to community are built into the very structure of society, through institutions and policies that deny the humanity of some communities and exclude them from full participation in civil society. These barriers can be seen as systemic harms and include, for example, sexism, racism, ableism, and classism. They are evident in inequities in access to employment, healthcare, education, housing, childcare, and healthy food, not to mention disproportional experiences with the criminal legal system and mass incarceration. These systems of dehumanization arise from, cause, and reinforce cycles of violence and marginalization among individuals and communities.

It is impossible to discuss every possible type of structural barrier here, so we will focus on white supremacy and structural racism because of their pervasiveness and the way they ground all other forms of oppression. After an introduction to white supremacy through the lens of the first and second harms, we explore how this orientation influences our thinking and behavior today and how it has resulted in collective and intergenerational trauma, both of which interfere with community.

The First and Second Harm

White supremacy is based on the false narrative that there is a hierarchy of human value based on racial identity, such that race is a social construction. When white settlers came to what has become the United States, they believed that they were superior to Native Americans, who already occupied the land and had for centuries. Through the doctrine of discovery, which "established a religious, political, and legal justification for colonization and seizure of land not inhabited by Christians,"[4] Europeans stole Native American land (an integral part of their community), treated them as less than human, stripped them of their culture, and forced them to assimilate. White settlers committed physical and cultural genocide from a worldview of white supremacy.

This genocide is often considered the "first harm." The enslavement of Africans by white settlers could be called the "second harm." When brought to the United States, they too were stripped of their culture, families, and homeland. Both Native Americans and the descendants of African enslaved people continue to suffer from the effects of systemic harm, such as racial discrimination in schools and workplaces, redlining, and disproportionate representation among crime survivors and people who are incarcerated.

Thinking and Behavioral Patterns

White supremacy is not confined to the past or limited to social policies. The practices of othering and dominance in the first and second harms can all be traced into the present, permeating day-to-day thinking and behavioral patterns of people of all skin colors in the United States. For example, white supremacist thinking includes adversarial and "us versus them" ways of operating, where there must be a winner and loser for every issue and a "right way" and/or a "wrong way" for every challenge. It is evidenced in insistence on efficiency and urgency, believing that both time and resources are scarce. It shows up in hyper-individualism, shameless self-promotion, wealth hoarding, and saviorism. It can also be found in tendencies of helplessness, avoidance, or the denial of problems. These harmful narratives, which contribute to division and marginalization, are seen structurally as well as in microaggressions and interpersonal violence, including (but not limited to) sexual abuse, domestic violence, psychological and spiritual abuse, cyberbullying, and financial harm.

Trauma

The first and second harms and the modern white supremacy orientation have contributed to structurally induced trauma that has broad and lasting impacts for many communities. *Trauma* is an occurrence or condition that overwhelms an individual or group's ability to cope or respond to threat,[5] often resulting in the fight, flight, freeze, and, more recently articulated, fawn and flop responses. Though each person's response to trauma varies (even when exposed to the same occurrence or condition) and is shaped by factors such as culture, environment, and prior experience, there are common reactions. Someone may act out toward others in productive or unproductive ways (causing violence toward others, running from danger, advocating for justice, or reaching out in assistance). Other times, someone may direct these energies toward themself, potentially to their own detriment (drug and alcohol abuse, insomnia, or physical activity). When trauma goes unhealed or unaddressed, it can perpetuate or escalate cycles of violence and self-harm. However, there are also healthy responses to trauma that can generate cycles of healing, repair, and possibly even movement toward reconciliation.

There are many types of trauma, and minds often go first to events that impact individuals, such as a car wreck or violent crime. When operating at the structural level, trauma can also be experienced collectively and intergenerationally. Collective trauma refers to when a group experiences a traumagenic event together and synchronously pauses, responds, and changes as a result. Global examples include wars and genocide, famine, COVID, and the Holocaust, while US-based ones include the assassination of Dr. Martin Luther King, the 9/11 attacks, the murder of George Floyd, or Hurricane Katrina. Intergenerational trauma occurs when violence enacted against a person or group has rippling impacts into the present; the violence itself may continue through the generations, or the trauma response may be passed down to descendants physiologically through physical illness, mental illness, or dysfunctional relationships. This can be seen, for example, in families with histories of abuse.

The aftermaths of the first and second harms are both examples of collective and intergenerational trauma. Both impacted whole societies of people (collective) and the impact has been passed down to descendants (intergenerational). For example, Black Americans' reactions to police stem from slave patrols in the 1700s, which set a precedent of terror and control. The patrols used excessive force to get compliance from enslaved people, behaviors which are documented in police brutality toward Black people today around the United States. A prime example is the murder of George Floyd, who, while pleading for his life, was crushed from the weight of an officer putting a knee on his neck and eventually murdering him. As Floyd called for his mother, he looked for the person who brought him into the world to save him. That time would never come for him.

The Equal Justice Initiative's Community Remembrance Project sheds light on the legacy of lynching by collecting soil from sites of violence, erecting markers, and maintaining a national monument in Montgomery, Alabama. One marker remembers Dana Adams, a Black man lynched near the Union Pacific depot in Saline County on April 20, 1893.

Adams was asked to leave a Salina train station, arrested after an altercation, and quickly sentenced to prison without representation. While being transported, a white mob intercepted the train and lynched him. Though only a few carried out the act, hundreds stood by in silent agreement. His father later sued the city, which offered him just two dollars—never acknowledging its role.

For Black residents, fear of community-wide retaliation kept them from intervening. The result was deep, generational trauma that endured for decades. Adams's death is a stark reminder of the cost of silence. Some in that crowd may not have wished him harm, yet they chose to say nothing—a choice that surely haunted them.

Responding to these historic harms and the resulting collective and intergenerational trauma is a difficult and complex issue. The traumagenic events and their impacts cannot be erased. Even so, conditions can be created for healing and security that interrupt harmful cycles and create new pathways for reconnection and creative possibilities. Such conditions support impacted individuals and communities to make meaning of the lost and devalued lives and to be seen and valued as equals by others—to experience belonging. The historical marker dedication for Dana Adams (see story in box) and the public apology from community officials is an amazing demonstration, a start, of what can happen when communities work together toward their healing.

Conclusion

These interpersonal and structural barriers to community make it challenging to carve out a path toward repair in the face of conflict and harm that does not further tear apart the community. Restorative justice offers a way through these barriers in order to hold those who cause harm accountable, support those who were harmed, and invite community members to support both.

Chapter 4
Restorative Justice

Dr. King's definition of justice foreshadows restorative justice. His core vision of creating the beloved community is closely akin to the relationship and community building that is at the heart of all restorative practices.

—Fania Davis[1]

What comes to mind when you hear the words "restorative justice"? Perhaps you envision a facilitated dialogue between a person in prison and the people they harmed or students participating in a circle process after an incident at school. These are just two of many potential examples of restorative responses to crime or rule violations. Restorative justice, however, is more than just dialogues after wrongdoing. It is a broad-reaching philosophy that can guide the ways we respond to and prevent potential harm in all aspects of our lives. Restorative justice offers ways to create space for listening and empathy, attend to tensions because of difference, and respond to systemic oppression, all while responding to harm. This chapter introduces the restorative justice philosophy and principles, considers its core values, and reviews key practices, with a particular eye to community perspectives and engagement.

Restorative Justice Philosophy

At the heart of restorative justice is an assumption that people desire and deserve to live in right relationships with one another, relationships that honor the inherent worth of every person and recognize that we are integrally connected in a web of relationships, whether we realize it or not. Harm-doing, be it interpersonal, criminal, or systemic, violates this wholeness, connection, human dignity, and relationships. The impact of harm-doing ripples out to those not directly involved. For example, after a burglary occurs at one home, neighbors may step up their home security or parents may warn their children not to play in that area, even though they were not directly impacted.

Restorative justice seeks and builds pathways for understanding and relational repair for those both directly and indirectly impacted or involved in harm. It does this by understanding the depth and breadth of the experience of the person who has been harmed and centering their needs (harmed party) and by including the person who caused harm (responsible party) and the community. For the responsible party, accountability takes the form of responsibility for one's actions and making amends for the harm that was done. Further, because restorative justice recognizes that every person has the potential to both suffer from and cause harm and that "hurt people hurt people," a restorative approach acknowledges that a responsible party may also have needs that require attention or harms that need repair.

Likewise, community members experience harm and carry responsibility in their own unique way. The harmed party, responsible party, and community may actually rely upon one another on the journey of repair and accountability.

Retributive versus Restorative Justice

As logical as it may be, the restorative justice approach stands in contrast with the way that many people and institutions understand and enact justice. The criminal legal system attempts to put people into categories of "victim" and "offender" or "guilty" and "innocent," ignoring the complexity of harm and harm-doing. Instead of relational repair, justice is typically retributive, where punishment is meted out so the harm-doer "pays what is due" for violating a rule or law. Such punishment typically results in confinement, isolation, removal of rights, or public shaming. This punitive orientation manifests in the legal system (incarceration), in schools (detention, suspension, or expulsion), in the workplace (summary dismissals), and in social settings (cancel culture). Surely, there are times that a person may need to be separated from a group for their own safety or that of others. However, problems arise when we impose suffering that further dehumanizes and neglects to address the causes of and needs created by the original harm.

Howard Zehr, renowned restorative justice scholar, clarifies the differences between a retributive and restorative approach with the following questions.

Retributive Questions	Restorative Questions
1. What law was broken? 2. Who is guilty? 3. What should their punishment be?	1. What was the harm? 2. Who was impacted and how? 3. What needs to be done to make it right?

A key distinction to note in these questions is that the retributive questions focus solely on the person who caused harm, whereas the restorative questions prioritize the person who was harmed. The retributive questions exemplify how those who were harmed often feel sidelined, if not revictimized, by the justice process. This marginalization typically means their needs are ignored and meaningful repair is absent. The restorative justice questions seek to put their needs and the repair of harms at center stage.

Restorative Justice Questions

Zehr further expands these "restorative questions" to more thoroughly reflect on a harm and guide a restorative justice response. These questions include:

1. Who has been harmed?
2. What are their needs?
3. Whose obligations are these?
4. Who has a stake in this situation?
5. What are the causes?
6. What is the appropriate process to involve stakeholders in an effort to put things right and address underlying causes?[2]

These questions are applicable for people who identify as a harmed person, a responsible person, and community members alike. Those who have been harmed will possibly get a deeper understanding of needs and ways to repair harm, while the person who caused the harm might benefit from a more in-depth understanding about obligations and ways to take responsibility for causing the harm. While these questions carry practical answers for those who are directly impacted by or involved in harm or a restorative justice process, they may be more reflective in nature for community members. We will expand upon these questions for community members in the next chapter because they are essential to reality-test your role in the community and assess whether and how to respond.

Restorative Justice Principles

Restorative justice can also be summarized in three basic principles, adapted here from Zehr's *Little Book of Restorative Justice*:

1. **Meeting needs.** Crime, harm and wrongdoing create needs. For the person harmed (harmed party), these needs may be for information, opportunities for growth, return of sense of safety, or repair of property. The person who caused harm (responsible party) also has needs, such as a pathway toward redemption and an opportunity to express remorse or to gain a sense of belonging and hope. Community members may have similar needs to each of these, depending on how they were impacted by or caused the harm.
2. **Obligations.** When harm happens, accountability occurs when the responsible party takes responsibility and makes amends to put

things right to the greatest extent possible. The community may have obligations as well, especially if the action or inaction of community members or institutions contributed to the underlying conditions of the harm itself, such as when a community member turns a blind eye to another's inappropriate behavior or social conditions that contribute to poverty and violence.

3. **Engagement.** Restorative justice relies upon the active involvement of the people most directly impacted, such as the harmed and responsible parties. It strives to include them in the process, but may not always do so. In other words, those closest to the problem ought to be closest to the solution. Engagement may also include those who are indirectly involved, such as community members. This engagement may take many forms, with facilitated dialogue between the harmed and responsible parties as just one form (we discuss this and others below).

The concept of restorative justice resonates with many people and is often described as being rooted in the values with which many of us were raised. It also spans cultures. For example, Chief Justice Emeritus Robert Yazzie of Navajo nation speaks to the importance of relationships and community when responding to harm-doing in the Navajo community:

> What is an offender? It is someone who shows little regard for right relationships. That person has little respect for others. Navajos say of such

> a person, "He acts as if he has no relatives." So, what do you do when someone acts as if they have no relatives? You bring in the relatives! Victim's rights [are] an important issue. What do you do about them? There too, you bring in the relatives![3]

"Bringing in the relatives" implies that we are all one human family and are therefore responsible for one another's well-being. If we take the principle of engagement seriously, then living in right relationship with one another, as a community, means finding ways to relate with people with whom we are at odds and relying on the support of others in the process.

Restorative Justice Values

A common way of talking about restorative justice is through the language of values—the moral and ethical guideposts that shape our thinking, behavior, and personal convictions. Restorative justice values help us to be our best selves and live in right relationship with others and are used to guide a restorative response. There are many restorative values, and we are highlighting just ten of them here.

A restorative approach recognizes that by nature of being human, every person has inherent *dignity* and is worthy of *respect*. This can be difficult to honor, especially when someone has acted in a way that is less than dignified, but it is important to remember that a person is more than the harmful thing they have done. Through a lens of restorative justice, *accountability* is understood as taking *responsibility* for our actions when we cause harm, being honest about what happened and its impacts. Closely connected with accountability is *amends*, making plans for concrete actions that can help to *repair* the material and relational harm. Each of these values contribute to *interconnectedness* and meaningful *reintegration* with the community, for both harmed and responsible parties. Ultimately, these values seek to build an environment where *healing* and *transformation* are possible—for individuals, communities, and systems.

Restorative Justice Values

- Respect and Dignity
- Responsibility and Accountability
- Repair and Amends
- Reintegration and Interconnectedness
- Healing and Transformation

Restorative Justice and Community

Though harmed and responsible parties are the central stakeholders in restorative justice, the community has a vested interest in harm-doing and responses to it because community members may find themselves engaging with the harmed and responsible parties. Additionally, some community members may feel impacts of the harm in their own unique way, as secondary or vicarious victims. Separate from serving as a support person, community members' dignity, sense of safety, well-being, or relationships may be violated.

This feeling may be because of their physical or relational proximity to people who were harmed or it may stem from sharing a sense of belonging with people who are directly impacted and thus also carry the weight of the harm. For example, Black, Indigenous, and other people of color (BIPOC) may be vicariously harmed when learning about police violence against unknown members of the BIPOC community. Additionally, each person has their own history of having caused and suffered harm. Not only can these experiences be reignited (consciously or subconsciously) when witnessing a new harm or knowing someone who has been harmed, they can also greatly shape the way a person reacts. Community members may also carry some level of responsibility for the behaviors or conditions that led to the harm.

Given this complexity, it is not always clear how to understand a community member's part in or reaction to the harm. When community members can identify their "lane" in proximity to the harm and directly impacted parties, they are better equipped to respond in a restorative way. Here, we introduce four "lanes."

Witness the Harm

There are many types of witnesses who experience the issue or harm firsthand. Witnesses who were physically present and witnessed harm in some way may be members of the community in which the harm occurred or they may be people who are thrust into the community by virtue of their proximity to the harm when it occurred. In an increasingly digitized world, witnesses may include those who observe the harm secondhand, through social media and other online forms of communication, such as watching live footage of a tragic event or observing harassment in a comment thread. Whether in person or online, sometimes bystanders may simply observe and choose not to act. Sometimes they step in and intervene to stop harm-doing or de-escalate rising tensions. Other times, unfortunately, bystanders involve themselves by intentionally provoking the situation, causing additional harm, or refusing to come to the aid of the harmed party or hold the responsible party accountable. In these incidents, their action or inaction makes them complicit in the harm-doing. All of these witnesses carry their own stories of impact. Despite this fact, witnesses need to understand that there is a difference between being indirectly harmed and being at the center of the harm.

> While sitting in traffic, I witnessed a vehicle hitting a bicyclist. I quickly pulled over and grabbed a blanket from my trunk for her to sit on while we awaited the ambulance. I asked someone to get her water at a nearby restaurant. I quickly assessed her other needs and called her loved ones to let them know what happened. Her partner quickly arrived and took over. I packed up our "camp" to a chorus of "thank you!" and went on my way.
>
> I didn't think about what I'd done as being a good bystander and support person. I just thought about what I'd need if I were in the bicyclist's shoes. However, not everyone thinks that way, and I wish that I could say that I always behave that way.
>
> —Sheryl

Support Harmed and/or Responsible Party

Community members may need to walk with people in the aftermath of harm in various capacities. Family members or neighbors may become caregivers to harmed or responsible parties or their children, when a parent is absent due to violence, incarceration, or recovery. In other circumstances, one might offer support helping to meet basic needs like making a meal, providing financial support, or housecleaning. A community member in this support role may have difficulty recognizing and attending to their own needs in relation to the harm, because the person who bore the larger brunt of the harm has more obvious needs. In this case, it is important to seek out resources for support (such as the Caregiver Action Network).

Respond in a Professional or Formal Capacity

Some individuals engage with harm because of their formal or professional capacities, making them both community members and people who serve the community. First responders, such as emergency medical professionals, firefighters, police officers, and victim advocates, step in. Therapists, social workers, and clergy may provide support in the healing process. Legal actors, such as judges, lawyers, and correctional officers, may become involved to manage, determine, or oversee the response to the harm. Elected officials, journalists, or business owners may mobilize resources and relationships in the service of recovery and accountability. These individuals are impacted by what they witness or learn firsthand from both harmed and responsible parties and secondhand from each other. These roles are important and sometimes absolutely necessary. However, overreliance on them has the potential to marginalize and disempower, and thus harm, some community members. It is critical to discern how to engage with them in the support of healing.

Carry Direct or Indirect Responsibility for Harm

Community members may, knowingly or unknowingly, contribute to the harm through actions or complicity, which can make it easy to deny responsibility and place blame solely on the responsible party. They may feel indirectly responsible because of their physical or relational proximity to the responsible party (such as a parent or sibling) or have a similar professional, cultural, or ideological identity, contributing to guilt by association. In other instances, when adjacent to harm, witnesses may fail to act or advocate for someone who has been harmed. For example, mandated reporters may fail to report issues of harm.

Restorative Practices for Community

Restorative practices are the means by which to answer the questions, apply the principles, and put the values into action. These voluntary processes aim to facilitate restorative outcomes such as rebuilding trust, increasing understanding, and repairing harm. They are often, but not always, dialogic, bringing people into conversation. Because restorative practices focus on people and relationships first, before addressing issues or attempting to make plans, they tend to get people to open up, practice empathy, let go of personal agendas, and allow new paths forward to emerge. Ideally, they are trauma-informed (sensitive to how past harms may impact a person's present-day experience) and resilience-focused (seeking to identify and build upon sources of strength and healing). As communities embrace being trauma-informed and resilience-focused, they will naturally gravitate toward processes that affirm restorative practices. There are numerous restorative practices, and we are highlighting just three that are especially community-oriented: victim-offender dialogue, circle processes, and truth and reconciliation commissions.

Victim-Offender Dialogue

Victim-offender dialogue (VOD) is a facilitated dialogue process that allows harmed and responsible parties to meet face-to-face in a structured conversation, guided by a trained facilitator. Usually initiated by the harmed party, VOD's focus is on how to handle things in the aftermath of crime or wrongdoing, offering an opportunity for the responsible party to be accountable and supporting the harmed party's healing journey. For example, the harmed person(s) has an opportunity to name all the ways that they were impacted by the harm, express their feelings, and/or request restitution from the person who caused the harm. They can be as creative as possible in how they recover. It is important to note that VOD facilitators do not bring their own agendas to the dialogue; rather, they allow for the needs of the harmed party to drive the process. With this practice, community members are typically involved as support people for those on both sides of the harm.

Circles

Rooted in centuries-old wisdom borrowed from First Nations, Native Americans, and Indigenous peoples from the northern US and Canada, circle processes "look at ways to be in good community with one another, so that if and when harm occurs, we have a foundation that we've built to repair it."[4] In circle processes, members of the community or group in dialogue sit in a physical or virtual circle and, after agreeing to shared guidelines, pass a talking piece around to signal the speaker. Circles typically begin and end with a ceremony and include other elements such as discussing individual values and offering discussion prompts that cover the topics important to all participants.

Circles are highly versatile in application and purpose. One of the most common circles is for community building so people get to know each other. By slowing down and responding to introspective prompts, participants discover things about one another that they might not otherwise know. Communities engaged in a discernment process regarding an issue may participate in problem-solving circles. In such a circle, everyone discusses their challenges and, once again, slows down so they hear each other differently than in other settings. A harm-repair circle may resemble a victim-offender dialogue in that it is an opportunity for the harmed and responsible parties to discuss the harm and its repair. Circles are different, however, in that all people present in the circle are participants and there is not an opportunity for an isolated dialogue between the harmed and responsible parties.

Truth and Reconciliation Commissions

Truth and reconciliation commissions (TRC) offer one of the best responses when harm is historical, systemic, or institutional in nature. TRCs are multiphase processes in which a commission, composed of representatives from various constituent groups from the community, identifies and addresses past harms, wrongdoings, and human rights abuses committed in society, usually under authoritarian rule. Both harmed parties and responsible parties give testimony before the commission to describe the harm and its impacts and take responsibility for their actions, respectively. TRCs usually provide findings from investigations, and from those findings, the commission offers a set of recommendations for the community to follow, as a means of repairing past harms.

Perhaps the most familiar TRC is the 1996 South African Truth and Reconciliation Commission, which grappled with what to do about the human rights abuses in the aftermath of apartheid, a forty-six-year implementation of racial segregation. The process began with a lengthy investigation as well as engagement with and testimony from those who were harmed (usually referred to as witnesses) and those who caused the harm (or perpetrators). After that, the commission started the daunting task of agreeing on consequences for responsible parties. Of the 7,000 amnesty applications from perpetrators and from the 2,500 amnesty hearings, 1,500 perpetrators were granted amnesty for thousands of crimes committed during the apartheid years.[5] Unfortunately, critics of the South African TRC felt that the commission did not go far enough to hold those who committed harm accountable for their actions.

In the United States more recently, the Maine Wabanaki-State Child Welfare Truth and Reconciliation Commission addressed issues involving the treatment of Wabanaki children and their families in the Maine child welfare system from 1978, when the Indian Child Welfare Act passed, until 2015. The process focused on the disproportionate rate of removal of Wabanaki children from their families. The findings revealed that Wabanaki children were removed from homes and placed in the foster system five times as often as non–Native American children. The commission placed decolonization at the heart of its process of reconciliation and introduced a new approach to healing for generations of Native people suffering from historical trauma.[6]

> In 2009, I provided support for those in the US diaspora giving testimony during the Liberian Truth and Reconciliation process hearings held at Hamline University in St. Paul, Minnesota. Each person shared their heartbreaking stories of genocide, rape, loss of property, and other collateral damages of the war and journey to the US. I will never forget the comments of one of the men I accompanied following his testimony: "I did it." He wept and bowed his head, as he reflected on how much sharing his testimony took out of him. I felt so honored to bear witness in this capacity.
>
> —Sheryl

Conclusion

Restorative justice offers an orientation and processes for harm repair that restores relationships among those who have been harmed, those who caused harm, and the community. In doing so, it also offers a way to be in right relationships with each other as a community, at the ready to respond when harm happens. The restorative framework can thus help individual community members navigate their own personal response to harm and accompany others in a similar way. In the next chapter we will explore what happens when restorative justice is employed in a community setting.

Chapter 5
Responding When Harm Occurs in Community

There are times when it is legitimate to avoid situations because they feel unsafe, of course. But let's be careful not to use this excuse to avoid the hard work that we must do if we are to become the "beloved community."

—Howard Zehr[1]

Restorative justice principles, values, questions, and practices can guide the community response to harm. But how does one get started with a restorative justice response? This chapter explores how to use the restorative justice questions to guide an individual community member's response to a harm and how one might engage in restorative justice practices.

Restorative Justice Questions

Regardless of the "lane" in which one finds themself in relation to the harm, people may feel uncertain about how to respond to Zehr's restorative questions. However, responses to these questions may help with clarifying one's connection to harm. Here, we wish to expand upon the questions that a community member may ask themself in the aftermath of harm. They may serve in preparation to support a loved one through a restorative justice process, but they can also apply to walking with directly involved parties regardless of the legal or community-based process that takes shape. These questions can also be helpful for community members seeking to process their experiences together.

A: Consider your experience

As noted in the previous chapter, there are several ways in which a community member may be impacted by or connected to a harm. That connection creates needs, making it valuable to assess and attend to those needs. This self-awareness becomes especially necessary when providing support to someone who was directly harmed or when we feel responsible for helping to repair harm. Journaling or meditating with these questions may be helpful, as may talking them through with someone you trust.

1. Assess what happened from your perspective

One cannot begin to respond to a harm without assessing its nature and extent. This assessment may be straightforward when someone is an eyewitness to the harm. Other times, it may be harder to recognize, such as when one learns about it secondhand or via social media. Questions to ask include:

1. What do I know or remember about what happened?

2. To what degree can I trust the source of information, and how can I ensure that what I know is accurate?
3. What, if anything, did I know about the potential of harm before it happened?

This is not a fact-finding mission. Rather, it is a way to gather what is known, to the extent possible, to form a cohesive narrative for yourself about what happened.

2. Explore the indirect impact on you and your needs
Once you have established an understanding of what happened, consider the impact of the harm on you and your subsequent needs. This awareness both supports you in meeting your needs and helps anticipate circumstances that might activate feelings that could render you ineffective later when engaging with a harmed or responsible party. Questions to consider include:

1. What was my reaction or response at the time of witnessing or learning of the harm? Reactions may be physically in one's body, mental, and/or emotional.
2. How do I feel now? How does it compare to my initial feeling?
3. How has this harm affected me mentally, physically, emotionally, materially, or spiritually?
4. What needs do I have and what is available to me to meet those needs?
5. If I am feeling some responsibility for the harm, what obligations do I have and how can I meet those obligations?

6. What does my experience with the harm and my needs suggest about my ability to engage with the harmed and responsible parties?

Spending time with these questions can help us order what may feel like a tangle of thoughts and feelings and gain new clarity about our unique experience.

Common needs for community members may be similar to those of directly harmed parties, such as talking about what happened or reestablishing a sense of safety. Their needs may also align with the responsible party, because they see themselves in that person. Such a community member may feel a new desire to atone for past actions or reevaluate their involvement in similar behavior. It is important to remember that at this stage you are just evaluating and taking steps to address your own unique needs, not yet identifying or addressing the needs of those directly impacted by or involved with the harm.

Learn About the Variety of Trauma Responses

Trauma affects each person differently and can unfold over time, sometimes even taking the person experiencing them by surprise. Be mindful of how trauma responses may manifest in yourself and people with whom you are engaging.

B: Consider those directly impacted and involved

The restorative value of interconnectedness means

that we, as community members, have obligations to those who are directly impacted by or involved in the harm. An individual community member may feel connected to the responsible party, the harmed party, or both, raising questions about which relationship to prioritize. These questions can be further complicated if/when engaging with the criminal legal system and a community member, for instance, is called to give testimony in a trial, sentencing hearing, or parole hearing. While some people may be in a unique position to equitably accompany people on both sides, there are instances when one may need to choose. Being true to the values of restorative justice means that even when choosing a side, we hold the other with compassion. When uncertain about whom to support and how, we may access outside, trusted support people to get their perspective.

While you can never fully know another person's experience, the questions below assist in understanding, to the best of one's ability, how people have been impacted or involved in harm and guide your next steps. Remember that there is no single checklist or "right answer" of what to do next. By answering these questions, we may avoid overstepping into an area where needs are already being met and can serve as a productive resource where they are not. This list is not exhaustive; you may realize that other questions are necessary based on the people involved and the harm that occurred.

3. Assess the impacts and needs of the harmed party

To learn about the experiences and needs of the harmed party, consider the following questions:

1. What do I know about who was affected by the harm?
2. What needs have I heard the harmed party express?
3. If they haven't expressed needs, how can I anticipate their needs without burdening them?
4. What needs do I already see being met by other people, programs, or systems?
5. What needs may be going unmet and which ones can I address?

Keep the Persons Harmed at the Center

When engaging with the harmed party, be conscientious not to unload your own unprocessed pain on them. Seek support people who understand you and the context and can empathize in a productive way. Whenever possible, process pain, confusion, anger, or helplessness with these people, rather than expecting the harmed party to provide that support to you.

4: Assess the obligations and needs of the responsible party

To understand the experiences, obligations, and needs of the responsible party, consider the following questions:

1. What do I know about what may have been happening for the responsible party leading up to the harm?
2. What might they have been thinking/feeling at the time? What do I know about how they have been feeling since?

3. What expressed or unexpressed needs are apparent? Are any of them being met and by whom?
4. What might the responsible party's obligations be to the harmed party and the community? What are my responsibilities and obligations to them?

Speaking to Encourage

As we show up to help someone who has caused harm, sometimes we might project shame or our own agenda rather than be present for that person's own processing of the situation. When we speak to encourage, we set aside our need for "facts" and, instead, offer questions that are introspective.

5: Assess the engagement with human service and system professionals

It can be overwhelming for the harmed and responsible parties to work with system and human service professionals such as mental health providers, victim advocates, investigators, social workers, attorneys, and law enforcement. Having someone to help clarify things, interpret situations, or document information can be extremely helpful. What's more, interfacing with law enforcement and courts can range from stressful to traumatic, so having someone present who is less traumatized is important. Thus, supporting someone as they deal with systems and their representatives can be very important. Some questions to ask may be:

1. What are the default legal or procedural repercussions for this event and how are they playing out?
2. What rights and services are each person legally entitled to and do they have access to them?
3. What existing additional or alternative supports/programs may be available locally and are they aware of these?

6: Consider structural barriers

In many incidents of harm, there are underlying conditions that contribute. As community members, we can reasonably ask:

1. What larger systems or structures may have contributed to the harmful actions?
2. What unhealed trauma may have led to this harmful event?
3. How do I participate in these structures?
4. What happens if I decide not to help deal with structural barriers?

By considering these factors, we can more easily develop empathy for those involved and potentially identify opportunities to address the root causes of harm-doing. Owning our responsibilities as community members includes recognizing our participation in structures that contribute to harm and doing what we can to change those behaviors and structures.

C: Discern your roles and responsibilities

After moving through the preceding questions, we will be better prepared to decide when and how to take steps to support the people and relationships impacted by and involved in the harm. In other words, it helps you understand your "lane" when it comes to responding to harm. The closer the relationship to the harmed or responsible party, the more prominent your role can be in helping to repair the harm. It may be that you can positively influence people in good ways to handle difficult situations or make phone calls to loved ones for the person you are supporting.

It is also important to gain the comfort and confidence to ask questions like "Would it be okay if I did [this]?" or "Can I take care of that for you?" A restorative approach calls us to always be aware of our responsibilities and to negotiate and reevaluate those responsibilities over time.

Remember Relational, Material, and Spiritual Supports

There are many ways to show support outside of one-on-one conversation. These can include informal actions such as, but not limited to, bringing meals or coordinating a meal train, serving as a proxy communicator for major updates, praying together, organizing a vigil, honoring event anniversaries, babysitting, transporting someone to the hospital, accompanying someone to court, and providing rides to significant appointments.

> One evening, my co-workers and I received a text from my colleague, Fr. Dustin. He had received a request to serve as spiritual advisor to a man scheduled for execution. Fr. Dustin would spend the next month sitting, talking, and praying with Jamie and his family, as his legal team worked through appeals. If needed, Fr. Dustin would be beside Jamie in the execution chamber.
>
> This was a path Fr. Dustin had walked before, so he was well-versed in the realities of vicarious and secondary trauma, often educating other prison chaplains about its impacts and resilience practices. He reached out because he knew that our staff understood the darkness of death row, outrage at the injustice, and the sacredness of his relationship with Jamie in all its complexity.
>
> Fr. Dustin invited us to be his circle of support so that he wasn't putting his needs (processed or unprocessed) on the shoulders of Jamie. In the process he invited us to draw closer to Jamie's story and humanity that was about to be discarded.
>
> —Caitlin

Community Roles When Formally Responding to Harm

The above questions prepare you to engage with harmed and responsible parties in meaningful and restorative ways. This engagement may be informal, through material, relational, or spiritual support, or more formal, such as through a victim-offender dialogue or coordinating other forms of facilitated communication such as letter-writing or shuttling communication back and forth between parties.

Engagement may be in the immediate aftermath of an event or years or even decades later. When a restorative response takes the form of a dialogue, there are particular roles that community members can play.

There is not enough that can be said about those in the community who are in roles as support people. These individuals accompany others in the aftermath of harm in emotional and practical ways. This may be a "go-to" friend or family member who gets the first call that something terrible has happened. It may also be someone who volunteers to assist when they recognize a need. That said, keep in mind that uninvited support is not always welcome. Before assuming responsibility for assistance, a capable support person will first check with or ask the directly impacted person about what they need. Sometimes people are able to choose how they can support a harmed or responsible party because of their preexisting relationship. For example, a neighbor can decide that they have the bandwidth to bring over groceries or prepare a meal. On the other hand, a bystander may not be afforded time to make specific decisions. Beyond attending to practical or material needs, support people recognize the value of listening and are respectful when someone communicates that they do not desire the kind of support that they are offering.

Community Members as Dialogue Participants

Everyone involved in a formal process of repairing the harm is considered to be a participant. This includes community members, be they a person facilitating restorative dialogue or those adjacent to the harm (witnesses, bystanders, neighbors, etc.). When involved in a restorative dialogue, community participants will be able to speak to how they were impacted, state what their needs are as a community member, express emotions, and contribute to the creation of an agreement to repair the harm. Community members may also be asked to participate in preparatory or follow-up conversations with the facilitator. They may bring their own unique concerns, needs, and desires, and may also serve as a representative of the wider community.

Support People for Dialogue Participants

VODs, circles, and TRCs call for support people to be there for the harmed and responsible parties. Often, there may not be clarity in how a community member should show up. In some cases, the support person might join the harmed and/or responsible party in the preparation process before the dialogue itself. They should be respectful of instructions about when to arrive, where to sit, and how best to share from their experience. They might offer to drive or travel with the person they are supporting or bring snacks or other items to help the person they are supporting to feel comfortable. Along the way, they remember that they are not the person closest to the harm, despite the fact that they may have suffered from or contributed to the harm themself. If they need to process their own harm or responsibility, they do that in a way that does not detract from the dialogue process itself.

In a restorative dialogue in its many forms, it is typically up to the most directly impacted persons to identify who they wish to participate in the dialogue with them. If someone you know asks you to support them, consider doing so, even if it feels intimidating. Outside of the dialogue itself, you can also be a listening ear to hear how it went, check in from time to time, and honor important milestones or anniversaries. Support people are comfortable with deep listening, asking open-ended questions, and refraining from pushing their own agendas or expectations.

Facilitators as Community Representatives

Dialogue facilitators are community members themselves—either as people that regularly engage with the community in which the harm occurred or individuals who simply feel a shared humanity with those who are harmed or harm-doers. By virtue of this, they too have a stake in the situation. By nature of being human, restorative processes do not assume that a facilitator can be 100 percent neutral. That said, in a VOD, the facilitator may maintain more of an objective stance, supporting the flow of the conversation, but not adding their personal experience or interpretation to the mix. In a circle process, the facilitator (sometimes called a circle keeper) is considered to also be a participant in the process, sharing themself in response to prompting questions. In all cases, a strong facilitator is mindful of their influence, able to remain emotionally regulated and put the needs of the group/participants first. Depending on the context, complexity, and intensity of the harm, different levels of experience are needed for facilitation. We encourage those who feel drawn to facilitation to pursue training in the broad or specialized skills needed to facilitate restorative processes in your context.

Facilitator Support People

The process of preparing for, facilitating, and debriefing a dialogue can be arduous, time-consuming, and emotionally taxing. Much like the impacted persons or community participants, facilitators often seek conversation partners as they process questions, reflect on experiences, and build skills. While the facilitator will not be able to share case details because of confidentiality, a support person can still offer a listening ear and remember them during the day or in, for instance, a personal meditative practice. It can be useful for a support person to set a reminder to check in with a simple "How are you doing?" throughout the dialogue process.

Surrogate Dialogue Participants

In the absence of immediate support people (who are willing and able to participate in a restorative dialogue), other community members can "stand in" as fellow neighbors invested in the well-being of the people involved in the community as a whole. In some cities, members of local churches and community groups participate in circle process training and then volunteer to participate when additional community representatives are needed. In addition to expressing their concerns, impacts, and needs, they may also serve as surrogate support persons to the harmed and responsible parties.

When direct dialogue is not possible or appropriate due to the preferences or availability of one party, surrogate participants who have been party to the same type of crime may step in to participate. For example, an individual who experienced a sexual harm may meet with a surrogate participant who committed and has taken responsibility for a sexual harm. Although these types of dialogues are not mainstream, with appropriate preparation and skilled facilitation, participants report high rates of satisfaction, especially harmed parties.

Administrative Support People

Most dialogue programs have a paid administrator of some kind to handle logistical coordination of communication, room setup, food, materials, or technology so that the participants and facilitator can be wholly present to the process. That said, there are many people who have administrative talents who might offer these to the community in a volunteer capacity. An administrator is adept at recognizing and fine-tuning the details that others may overlook (such as room temperature, accessibility for persons with disabilities, and dietary restrictions) in order to ensure that attention remains on the dialogue, rather than logistical distractions. Someone within this role might intuitively notice where they can attend to these needs in the background.

Professional or Formal Roles

As stated earlier, some community members have professional or formal roles through which they serve the community. These people may be working in the criminal legal system, medical system, or community service agencies. People who are already in or considering entering one of these professional roles can consider ways to remain in good and right relationship with the community being served and how, in their professional capacity, they can support opportunities for restorative justice when harm happens.

In some cases, relationship building, education, and accompaniment may be needed in order to invite and encourage restorative responses among people in professional roles, especially if they are not the norm in their context. Communities may also need to navigate the policies, regulations, and existing practices that support or limit the nature of system actors' involvement in a restorative dialogue. Nevertheless, system actors can play a valuable role in supporting and enabling restorative responses to harm in their communities.

Resource Navigator

Resource people are available when specific needs arise for community members. This person may hold professional expertise (such as a mental health counselor to provide therapy) or have skills and knowledge to make referrals to those who do (such as a social worker to connect with job services). This person may also be a community member without specific professional expertise but who is connected to additional resources through their own networks or may accompany someone who is connecting with services. A resource navigator may help identify local "wrap-around" services that attend to needs that may have contributed to the underlying conditions of the harm such as employment services, AA/NA groups, parenting groups, or housing assistance. They may also help connect harmed parties to medical providers or support groups.

Conclusion

The feelings, needs, and obligations of the directly impacted parties and community members will likely change over time. This means it is helpful to return to the guiding questions at multiple points in the healing journey. Roles and responsibilities will also likely change. Regardless of the specific role, people who support the people on either side of harm are invaluable resources to help navigate a path forward. Whether just being present, accompanying a harm-impacted person to court, or facilitating a dialogue, people in these roles are greatly appreciated.

Chapter 6
Restorative Community

Nothing is sweet or easy about community. Community is a fellowship of people who do not hide their joys and sorrows but make them visible to each other as a gesture of hope.

—Henri Nouwen[1]

We have shared about barriers to communities and opportunities for restorative responses within them when harm occurs. This leads us to becoming restorative communities (RCs). Applying restorative justice to a community setting is not just about how we respond to harm. It is also about minimizing the barriers to community and bringing about new norms, expectations, and belonging. Along the journey, we must tend to the space of "in between" where, even amid connection, harm and inequity exist, as does healing and repair. To be clear, an RC can be any type of community that chooses to act in a restorative way. Such communities may also organically form around culture, experience, location, interests, or beliefs. In the midst of hardship, our communities can help us reconnect with ourselves and others, as well as with a sense of purpose, belonging, and hope. In this chapter we will discuss what an RC is and principles for creating one.

Restorative Community

Restorative communities do what is possible to prevent harm and to heal harm when it does occur. They do this with a grounding in restorative justice. This means that a community:

- Is oriented toward right relationships, equal respect, and care, and serves as a guiding light for how members relate to one another and systems function
- Sees belonging as recognition that each person has needs and obligations that need to be met and that engagement is central to meeting them, especially when community members have been impacted by an issue or harm
- Abides by values such as trust, healing, repair, collaboration, interconnection, and interdependence
- Seeks to repair harm restoratively, supporting those who have been harmed and holding accountable those who cause harm

By following these principles and values, RCs minimize barriers to community by practicing listening and empathy, engaging with difference, and mitigating structural barriers. RCs recognize that every person has the potential to both suffer and cause harm, and no one person has all the answers for how to move forward. Members of these communities recognize that they do not get it right every time, take ownership when mistakes happen, and agree to fumble, search, and grow together, rather than retreating to polarized sides.

Being a part of an RC can help to reprogram the settings within ourselves that default to disconnection, isolation, and social silos. They help us learn how to be more empathetic, compassionate, and forgiving people with others and with ourselves. They teach us that vulnerability and accountability are not to be feared, but rather welcomed and perhaps even sought out. This helps us to embrace that we are all wounded in one way or another and that these wounds can be a source of strength and healing for others. Because of this, they teach us to notice, name, and engage with conflict instead of running from it. And when it comes to harm, RCs teach us that transformation is, in fact, possible.

A singular person or a collective of people may introduce these qualities to the communities they inhabit. Either way, there are group-oriented dynamics to take into account. A community's sense of purpose will certainly guide its choices and actions, but the best of intentions can be muddied by unclear expectations and unhealthy group dynamics. RC members choose to relate to people who are different from themselves because they recognize that our interconnectedness means that we all have a role to play in the solution.

Principles of Restorative Communities

RCs do not just happen on their own. They are created, often through intentionality on the part of their members, by meeting needs, considering obligations, and fostering engagement. Below, we introduce principles to build an RC and make it possible for any type of community to become a restorative one, whether it is an informal group interaction or a more formal one, like a meeting.

1. Lead with Values

In order to successfully build RCs and respond to harm restoratively, it is important for a community to identify its shared values. After identifying our personal or individual values, which strengthen how we show up in a community, we can determine whether or not these values align with the behaviors of others in the community. We can then determine areas of concern and, perhaps, carefully voice them. Conversely, the tension that exists between values may be helpful and even necessary in driving a powerful dialogue—allowing us to remain present with authenticity and lean into working toward finding areas of alignment.

2. Develop a Sense of Mutuality

A sense of mutuality is rooted in a belief that our well-being is integrally dependent upon the well-being of others, including people who see a situation or the world differently. It ushers in a means of joint decision-making, balance, and ultimately a sense of "we" instead of "I." Mutuality does not require agreement on an issue, but rather a recognition that we need one another to survive, thrive, and flourish. Realizing our interdependence can empower and bond people on both sides of an issue, whether it be navigating how to be good neighbors or having each other's backs in the wake of harm.

> Back in the day, my dad and his friend and neighbor Richard were low on resources. Between the two of them, they had six good tires for their vehicles. They were able to acquire one new tire that they shared. When my dad had to go to school in the morning, he put the tire on his car. In the afternoon, Richard would get the tire so that he could go to work. While this situation was short-lived, it offers a wonderful narrative: if being neighbors in our community is truly a mutual experience, then sometimes you're giving the tire, and sometimes you're the recipient of the tire!
>
> —Sheryl

3. *Bring an Asset Mindset*

It is all too easy to see people and communities through a lens of deficiency, focusing on what's missing, what needs fixing, or, even worse, blaming individual people for complicated problems. It is only natural to see deficiencies more clearly, especially in situations of harm. However, if we operate exclusively from this position, we get pulled into a vortex of negativity and despair.

Here lies an invitation to appreciate and build upon the goodness that is also present. Instead of focusing only on the deficiencies, identify the gifts, talents, and assets within ourselves, one another, and the group, and dedicate energies into leading from those places. In the wake of harm, this may be listing and even mapping material resources, skill sets, relationships, and lessons learned. A community can look back at what they have done well, the factors and conditions that led to success, and how that success may be replicated or leveraged to address current and future challenges. We can not only name and appreciate these successes, but also informally or formally celebrate them along the way.

4. Create Shared Agreements

When communities gather, its members often operate off unspoken assumptions, or a small group puts forth a set of norms or rules that they expect everyone else to follow. An RC creates shared agreements about how the community aspires to be present with one another and the world around them. Key elements around which to create shared agreements include:

- Values that undergird the community's choices, actions, and ways of being together;
- Behavioral expectations and norms that are in alignment with the shared values;
- Practices to be used when having difficult conversations, responding to conflict or harm, and making decisions in a way that is safe and honors the dignity and privacy of all;
- Guardrails that hold groups accountable to one another when agreements are broken.

These agreements are not used to browbeat one another; rather, they are invitational, supportive, and aspirational. They can be created using a circle process, where each person proposes guidelines and then the group discusses and comes to consensus on the final ones by which each will abide. It is important for a group to periodically revisit, amend, and reaffirm their commitment to the agreements.

Indeed, shared agreements may take on new layers of meaning and depth as the community matures. They may also be scaled in formality depending on the scope, length, or depth of the work. For example, an informal conversation between friends or colleagues probably does not need a written set of cocreated guidelines, but they could be brought up if the conversation goes sideways. Slightly more formally, a social media group may include a code of conduct survey that someone needs to agree to in order to join. More formality may be needed when an organization or coalition is figuring out how to work together toward a common mission.

5. Extend Welcome

In our experience, the communities and groups who commit to extending welcome have a certain magnetism. People on the peripheries may be drawn not to what the group is doing, but more so *how* they are doing it. Likewise, being welcoming prepares a group to become invitational in their style, rather than guarded, defensive, or exclusionary. This is not to say that a community may not need to articulate criteria or expectations. Part of the group's magnetism may be that the group has clearly discerned and defined their values and purpose. It is only reasonable to articulate these in a way that enables individuals to meaningfully consider their own engagement. The key to an invitational community is that its edges are penetrable enough to welcome a diversity of newcomers whose interests align with the best interest of the whole.

Sometimes, no effort is made at all to acknowledge the presence of a new person in a community or to orient them or consider what they add to the community. Other times, when a new person arrives, they are bombarded with requests and responsibilities without consideration for their hopes or needs. A restorative way to welcome someone to a group can be through public welcome as well as personalized conversations, where an established community member seeks to learn more about, for instance, the newcomer's background and interest in the group, hopes for joining, any concerns or questions they may have, and how they prefer to be addressed.

6. Learn through Listening

All communities engage in learning in some form, from working through a complicated issue to figuring out a new piece of technology. Many times, learning is assumed to occur through the presentation and memorization of information. Learners tend to look for the "right answer" from presenters. These speakers are often just the most confident ones and their involvement often silences the quieter voices.

In contrast, an RC incorporates listening into their learning and ensures that every person's voice, reflections, feelings, and fresh ideas are heard and honored. They build in time for personal reflection and create opportunities for each person to share how they connect with or are affected by an issue, allowing for a wider conversation about what this new or increased knowledge means for the group. Through deep listening and sharing, community members not only integrate the new information, but also build and strengthen relationships along the way.

7. Celebrate the Little Things

Following a successful project, event, or season, many communities acknowledge the obvious and big milestones through parties, flowers, cards, gifts, and formal ceremonies, but then move on to the next thing right away. RCs pause and take time to celebrate big and little achievements by the group and individuals. In addition to conventional gestures of acknowledgment, a circle process can be used to invite members to express what they are joyful and proud about, how they were personally touched by a person or event, and outstanding community contributions, as well as identify hurdles that they overcame and lessons learned along the way. They can also affirm one another and recommit to support and shared purpose going forward. These strategies can be applied following a milestone (anniversary, goal achieved, or event held) or in anticipation of one (birth of a baby or a significant move).

8. (Re)Connect

There can be a tendency in communities to think *we already know each other well enough* or *we have been doing this stuff together for a while.* RCs cultivate connection, trust, and belonging in groups, even when people know each other. There are numerous ways to do this. For example, the invitation to play, move, create, or try new things—such as with ice-breakers, games, or crafts—often stretches comfort zones, elicits creativity, and requires a certain level of discomfort and vulnerability that give way to new and deeper (re)connections. Members can create moments to pause and share stories or reflections about aspects of their lives outside of the typical group conversations. One may do this by checking in at the beginning of gatherings by asking, "How are you feeling as you arrive today?"

Such approaches can also be meaningful for the inevitable times of transition, structural change, and growth or shifts which may be accompanied by both joy and sorrow. For example, in moments of departure, each person can share how they were touched by the person leaving. In addition to symbolic gestures that acknowledge change, avenues can be created to involve group members in the changes that most impact them.

9. Support Each Other and Grieve Together

We get to choose how to respond when we ourselves, another community member, or group of community members is going through a hard time, whether they are overwhelmed, grieving, or suffering. We may think *I'll deal with it myself* or we might avoid, pathologize, or minimize a response. Instead, RC members prioritize physical and psychological safety and processes, such as circles, so that members may share how they are affected by the situation and process what happened (or is happening). These conversations allow for the catharsis of individual sharing as well as the surfacing of personal or community needs for moving forward. Such processes also build resilience, the ability to "successfully [adapt] to difficult or challenging life experiences, especially through mental, emotional, and behavioral flexibility and adjustment to external and internal demands."[2] With resilience, an individual may be able to bounce back after a traumatic, painful, or adverse event, such as a car accident, burglary, broken relationship, natural disaster, or neighborhood-wide crime. Fostering such resilience requires peeling back the layers of day-to-day interactions to understand one another's hurts, desires, and basic human needs so that we, as community, may be in a position to help meet those needs.

10. Use Consensus Decision-Making

Every community has times when they need to address challenging topics, solve problems, and make decisions. Too often, we rely on someone "at the top," in formal or informal positions of authority, to hand down a decision with the expectation that it be implemented without question, and without consideration of the experiences and wisdom of the people that the decision impacts most. Conflict often follows when people feel shut out in this way.

A remedy is to use horizontal approaches that bring people into the decision-making process and appreciate that every person has a different perspective on the issue and deserves to be heard. Talking pieces are one way to ensure that every person's voice is heard and considered. Another is consensus-based decision-making. In this approach, in the end, every person affirms that they can live with an agreement made by the group and carries shared responsibility for the follow-through. If there is a concern or dissent, the group works together to modify the plan until all can support the outcome. This approach can be more time-consuming and may bring up tension and disagreement, but when undertaken well, it can address the topic at hand in a way that is more widely supported and sustained. It may also cultivate resilience amid adversity as well as collaboration, coalitions, and cocreation, much like restorative practices.

When a consensus-based model is not feasible or appropriate, it should be clear who is responsible for making the decision and how group members' input will be taken into account. The key is to adopt a posture of listening, where the person or group in leadership actively and openly elicits the input of others, takes that input into consideration, and ensures that the end result is reflective of the input received. This includes exercises in accountability, where the deciding person or group is able to explain the decision as being rooted in the well-being of the whole. This is starkly different than simply taking a majority vote or blindly moving forward without consultation.

11. View Conflict as an Opportunity

In both informal day-to-day interactions and more formal gatherings, like meetings, all communities navigate hardship, conflict, injustice, stress, or uncertainty. In response, many of our minds and bodies default to "fight" (debate or convince) or "flee" (avoid or disengage from the conversation). We may deny responsibility, place blame, gossip about others involved, or attempt to scapegoat or outsource the problem.

RCs see conflict as an opportunity for engagement. While maintaining safety for all, they work to understand the experiences and divergent views of each party and find solutions that might meet the needs of all. Community members make the conscientious choice to get curious about the experiences of others and unfolding group dynamics. They stay nimble and open to a variety of perspectives and accept that they can still be in relationship with another person even when perspectives or values are not in alignment.

Engaging conflict in this way requires wondering about other people, their experiences, and perspectives as well as honoring their dignity. Like any disciplined athlete or performer, building this "wonder muscle" takes time. Circle processes are one approach that develops this muscle as they put relationships first, taking time to get acquainted and build trust before exploring a variety of possible next steps and agreeing on action items. This approach to conflict further develops individual and community resiliency.

12. Lead through Collaboration

In some cases, two communities may find that they share alignment around a particular goal or need, but maintain distinction in their core purpose, audience, or member identity. This can be a fabulous opportunity for collaboration. That said, there are two narratives that tend to interfere with collaboration: competition and transactionalism. Competition emerges when groups see other groups as a threat. This is often a reaction to perceived or actual scarcity in resources, power, or influence. With transactionalism, the motivation to be in a relationship with one another is because I need to "get" something from you or you owe me something. Typically, these sentiments are felt, but not named.

The counterweight to both of these is humility—the recognition that no one is perfect, complete, or all-knowing. By working together, we may complement one another to reach a common goal. In healthy collaborations, all groups remain committed to their respective missions and members while identifying a particular area of intersection to advance a common aim. For example, collaboration takes place when system-based entities refer cases to community-based organizations, or social work departments in higher education do work in community-based organizations. Collaborations between communities can take a variety of forms such as hosting events, combined advocacy, or joint programming. Groups may form formal or informal coalitions in which "all boats rise."

At times, a resource, policy, or program needs to be created. In this case, a community may lean into an ethic of cocreation. Like collaboration, cocreation acknowledges that a singular person or group will not have all the answers or knowledge necessary to generate that which is yet to exist. In cocreation, an individual or group may lead an initiative, but actively involve a diverse group of collaborators to inform and infuse the creative process from start (idea gathering and structural recommendations), to middle (crafting and piloting), to end (review and feedback). This ground-up approach stands in contrast to authoritarian, top-down approaches in which a singular person generates the idea, strategy, and deliverable and then expects others to support it without critique or question.

Cocreation is rooted in restorative justice practice in which the impacted persons cocreate a restitution agreement by suggesting potential reparative actions, and can be used to create restorative justice programs. For example, an informal coalition may form to advocate for a restorative process to happen in a particular case. A more formal cross-organizational coalition may be created to advance a restorative justice policy. The key is that each community participates in a way that brings their best selves to the shared work.

In 2012, Precious Blood Ministry of Reconciliation (PBMR) in Chicago, Illinois, initiated a pilot project with Cook County and a local judge to facilitate restorative circles with young people involved in the criminal justice system. When PBMR began to receive cases outside of their neighborhood, which they did not have the capacity to support, they sought out other neighborhood-based organizations with aligned missions to establish Chicago's RJ Hubs, "a collective that believes transformation is achieved when communities have the resources and capacity to resolve crime and conflict without the use of costly confinement and mass incarceration." Together, the early founders laid out five core pillars:

- Radical hospitality, providing a welcoming and hospitable place
- Accompaniment of youth and adults in their journey
- Building relationships with youth, adults, and family
- Relentless engagement of systems and stakeholders
- Learning community, collaboration, and learning with other RJ Hubs[3]

Fr. David Kelly, executive director at PBMR, recalls the group's members wrestling with the language and making revisions—all the while remaining committed to their shared focus on the young people and their needs and bringing as many organizations as possible to the table.

Bringing together two or more groups, organizations, or institutions around a common purpose can be difficult, as each arrives with their own sets of values, norms, and expectations that need to be considered and clarified (as is the case with individuals in a group). Think of how hard it is to turn around a ship in choppy waters. When it is done, however, it usually brings the vessel to calmer seas. With time, thoughtful consideration, and planning, groups can coalesce on areas of alignment, even if they do not agree on everything.

Conclusion

The above principles form a foundation of what it means to be in right relationship with one another, to be in a restorative community. The choice to slow down and engage relationally may not come easily, and crisis situations may require speedy responses. However, many things do not need to be done overnight in order to be done well. Further, all kinds of communities can become restorative ones—families, workplaces, schools, neighborhoods, churches, civic associations, and more. Perhaps you already see your own communities as being restorative or having restorative elements to them. Maybe it feels like they still have a way to go. When assessing a community's "restorativeness," one can appreciate and celebrate where these qualities are already in motion and initiate a plan to take next steps to becoming more fully restorative. There are also roles that each of us can play in order to build restorative communities.

Principles of a Restorative Community

1. Identify community values and examine how they shape group expectations, norms, and practices.
2. Look for ways to reflect upon interconnectedness, within and beyond the community itself.
3. Seek out ways to appreciate the goodness already present in a group.
4. Take time to develop shared agreements for general life in the community and for accountability processes.
5. Extend welcome and get to know newcomers.
6. Cultivate approaches for listening and learning that are participatory.
7. Pause and take time to celebrate the little things.
8. Embrace opportunities for community members to deepen their connections, even when people know each other.
9. Create processes for community members to safely share difficult experiences and what they need to move forward.
10. Whenever possible, use consensus-based decision-making to ensure that every person's voice is heard and considered.
11. View conflict as an opportunity to understand others' experiences and find solutions that meet the needs of all.
12. Seek out ways to collaborate with others who share a common goal, even if you do not agree on everything.

Chapter 7
Roles to Build Restorative Communities

The greatness of a community is most accurately measured by the compassionate actions of its members.

—Coretta Scott King[1]

Communities cannot move forward restoratively without the active participation of their members. It takes many people, with many gifts and talents, to support and build restorative communities. Individuals, subgroups, and groups in collaboration all play a role, each taking on particular responsibilities. There are formal roles and responsibilities we may choose to take on. And, especially in Black, Indigenous, and other communities of color, there are informal roles that are not assigned, articulated, or labeled. However roles are named or claimed, we each have unique wisdom, perspectives, and resources to bring to the table and a stake in the quality of our communities. Together, we can weave a resilient, responsive, and dynamic labyrinth of relationships that contribute to healing, accountability, and the well-being of all. This chapter discusses key formal, informal, and overlapping roles that people can play to build restorative communities and promote restorative justice.

Roles for Building Restorative Communities

We have mentioned the importance of knowing one's "lane" when it comes to harm and our responses to it. Here, we offer roles necessary to construct a restorative community. Naming and claiming these roles, for oneself and within the community, is essential to creating a restorative ecosystem of relationships. Equally important is *how* we fulfill these roles, in line with the values and principles of restorative justice.

Participant

When presented with an opportunity to participate in a community in any way, do it! Participate in games to get acquainted with others. Share from your experiences. Abide by community values and guidelines. Model deep listening and sharing. Add your wisdom to difficult conversations. Meaningfully reconnect with people you already know. Lead meetings differently. The whole community will benefit.

Facilitator

Formal and informal community gatherings of all sorts, including in response to harm, need trained facilitators who are appropriate for the type of engagement that is occurring. In simple community conversations, comfort and familiarity with leading group discussions may be enough, whereas in higher levels of harm or complexity, greater levels of skill, expertise, and training may be necessary. Depending on the situation at hand, it is important for the group to discern whether the person(s) facilitating should be existing member(s) of the community, someone external to the group, or a combination of both (in the case of co-facilitators), and whether the facilitator will also participate directly in the conversation itself, if appropriate, or solely lead others in their participation.

A facilitator may be the one to gather members together, or they may partner with other community leaders to convene the group. Regardless, the facilitator will listen closely and collaborate with community members to plan the process itself and ensure it meets the needs of the group. If participants are uncertain about their own contribution, a facilitator will take time to accompany individuals in preparation and follow-up. In a restorative community, the facilitator(s) will purposely use participatory processes to ensure that the contributions of all are welcomed and integrated. A facilitator in a restorative community is mindful of their own position of influence and puts the needs of the group first. They also invite and integrate feedback about the process itself and their own facilitation.

Convenor

Convenors are trusted people with a knack for gathering people together. They ensure that all those who have a stake in the outcome are present, especially people whose voices and perspectives have traditionally or historically been marginalized. They extend the personal invitations and articulate the value of that person's contribution to the process. Convenors are also skilled at developing generative group processes that allow for equitable participation, though they may or may not be the facilitator themselves.

Seed Planter

A seed planter is someone whose prior learning about restorative justice and practices has attuned them to see opportunities for its use. They may simply be the person who suggests that there may be a different way to approach a conversation, or they may be an educator or community leader who introduces restorative justice in their curriculum or community event. A seed planter does not need to be an expert in the field, but can draw from resources or experienced leaders to expand the knowledge and awareness of others.

Roles for Promoting Restorative Justice

There are also roles that individuals and groups can play in supporting and using restorative initiatives in the community and across a variety of settings. Whether setting up a restorative justice program, adopting restorative practices in schools, or addressing systemic barriers to healing and accountability, these roles add restorative touches in otherwise less-than-restorative environments. While discussed below as roles for individuals, some roles may be played by institutions through their programs and relationships with, for instance, seed planters, resource providers, and communicators. For example, Restorative Arlington, an organization with which Caitlin is involved, is in relationship with the prosecutor's office to receive case referrals. They also make formal and informal partnerships with schools, churches, community centers, and local businesses to spread the word and raise awareness about their efforts and invite engagement and collaboration.

Bridge Builder

A bridge builder is adept at recognizing common values and needs between groups, stakeholders, and initiatives in order to identify areas for collaboration that meet multiple groups' interests or to help clear a pathway among organizations in ways that cut through the bureaucracies that often divide organizations. Such a person is generous in making introductions that initiate new relationships and possibilities for coalition building. They are typically well connected both within and beyond the group and are resourceful and creative. They have an awareness of their own influence and are willing to share from their abundance in terms of time, resources, or skill in a way that elevates others along the way. A neighborhood bridge builder may be the person who serves as a neighborhood watch person. Instead of sitting on their porch ready to anonymously post violations on NextDoor, they hold genuine conversations with their neighbors, offer resources, or throw a block party.

Advocate

Advocates serve as supporters who undergird restorative practitioners. They are "friends of restorative justice" who are willing to enter into a relationship with people in power to voice their support for access to restorative solutions, while remaining accountable to the people and communities most impacted. In this role, one might contact legislators or participate in an active campaign. An advocate can also be a person using their influence to increase awareness and support. In doing so, the advocate also has a distinctly restorative approach.

When taking on the role of an advocate, one needs to be mindful of how cancel culture and social media have made it easy to "call people out" and assert that "they over there" should be doing things differently. Indeed, restorative justice practitioners have been gathering to address the harms regarding the phenomenon of cancel culture. A recent such gathering grappled with "how callouts could be a cry for change *and* reconciliation," and asked, "How do [practitioners] appreciate the underlying needs, while at the same time, offer worldviews in which resilience and compassion are central and strategic?"[2]

An adage from the nonviolent communication field may be helpful here—it says "connect before you correct." In a restorative community, an advocate is someone who makes this connection by seeking a point of common ground to build upon, rather than simply telling someone they are wrong or acting in an undesirable way. In groups, an advocate may open up a needed conversation either with the group or with a critical leader. This skill of getting to know one another as people, listening first before assuming intentions or asserting an agenda, is a critical skill for advocates. With increased trust and insight, the advocate can extend an invitation to consider a restorative approach and offer to be a resource.

Communicator

When there are stories of where and how restorative approaches have been successful within the community, a communicator may help document what transpired and, if desired, share the story for others, either within the community or beyond. This may be through social media, speaking publicly, video documentation, or writing an op-ed for a local news outlet. In addition to being skilled in journalism, public education, video production, or other technical skills, this person is attuned to the core values of restorative justice, seeks to honor the dignity of each person involved, and shares the story in a way that does not cause further harm to its subjects or the audience.

Evaluator

An evaluator assists the community in taking stock of how a restorative process or effort is going and identifying indicators of success, areas of significant learning, and opportunities for improvement, according to the people most directly involved. Some evaluation methods, such as Participatory Action Research (PAR), are well suited for evaluating restorative justice initiatives because they involve the immediate stakeholders in the design and implementation of the research itself.

The evaluator may be someone who is internal or external to the community. In their aims to reflect restorative principles, evaluators in a restorative community emphasize relationships, listening, and inclusion in their methods. These evaluators are not looking to extract information and share it in exclusionary ways. Rather, their approaches ensure that members of the community have full access to the learnings gleaned.

Conclusion

While embracing restorative approaches ultimately requires the attention and willingness of a whole group, they may be introduced by one person in particular. Anyone from the above roles can take up this charge. What is important is that building a restorative community is not the responsibility of a single person. Rather, it takes shape as each person brings their particular gifts and talents and collaborates with people in other roles to build trust and capacity to introduce ideas, initiate processes, and see commitments through.

You may already know that your skills, capacities, and relationships situate you for a particular kind of contribution. Perhaps you want or need to spend more time discerning your potential role. Maybe you see other roles not listed here, or move between several of them. Identifying these opportunities can help us appreciate, seek out, and work well with people who have strengths and capacity in roles different from our own. As you discern your role, remember that it is entirely possible, if not likely, that you may be skilled in multiple areas, and therefore may hold multiple roles. You will also have limitations, including in skills, time, and capacity. It is important to be mindful of both gifts and limitations to engage in the most meaningful ways possible.

No one person or group should be responsible for all of the roles needed to build restorative communities or promote restorative justice. It is not a reasonable expectation for anyone. Moreover, a core tenet of restorative justice is shared power and responsibility. If we, as community members, are to grow a restorative web of relationships, we need to create opportunities for people of many gifts and talents to be a part of the picture, all while abiding in the core principles of restorative justice.

Chapter 8
Restorative Self

If we do not transform our pain, we will most assuredly transmit it.

—Richard Rohr, OFM[1]

In order to respond to harm and contribute to the creation of a restorative community, it is important to grapple with our own experiences with being in community, barriers to community, being harmed, and causing harm. These personal experiences, positive and negative, shape our individual expectations for community—how we perceive their purpose, hope for them to function, and behave and relate within them. These experiences then influence our own tendencies or reluctance to respond to harm and people involved in or impacted by it.

Members of restorative communities reflect on our personal experiences and embody the lessons to develop a restorative inner being and way of living in community. One could think of this as "re-membering" community; that is, locating the parts and assembling them in a way that may or may not have previously existed. Such reflection can fuel personal journeys of healing and accountability, prepare oneself to deal with harm in restorative ways, and make it easier to support others around you. We are more likely to show up in communities as expressions of our best self and core values.

This chapter invites you to re-member community by engaging in personal self-reflection so you may realize how the personal experiences you carry may make it easy or difficult to develop a restorative inner being, embrace restorative responses to harm-doing, and contribute to a restorative community. After an introduction to Zehr's "Ten Ways to Live Restoratively," we offer guidance for this self-reflection.

We know that for some people self-reflection may feel uncomfortable, frightening, or downright impossible, especially for those whose memories are not positive. Therefore, you are invited to contemplate your experiences only to the degree they support you and offer new insights. However, the more we commit to self-reflection, the more easily it becomes part of the way we go about our day-to-day life. If this approach can become the default in small moments, it builds and stretches our ability to respond in similar ways when the stakes are higher.

Restorative Living

Howard Zehr offers a list of "Ten Ways to Live Restoratively,"[2] which proposes simple ways that every person can embrace the principles and values of restorative justice in their everyday lives. You will notice that all of these ways relate back to ideas and concepts presented in earlier chapters. Thus, reflecting on them and doing your inner work is core to being able to live out restorative justice values. These ten ways to live restoratively are the backdrop for the interior reflective work.

Ten Ways to Live Restoratively
(Howard Zehr)

1. Take relationships seriously, envisioning yourself in an interconnected web of people, institutions, and the environment.
2. Try to be aware of the impact—potential as well as actual—of your actions on others and the environment.
3. When your actions negatively impact others, take responsibility by acknowledging and seeking to repair the harm—even when you could probably get away with avoiding or denying it.
4. Treat everyone respectfully, even those you don't expect to encounter again, even those you feel don't deserve it, even those who have harmed or offended you or others.
5. Involve those affected by a decision, as much as possible, in the decision-making process.
6. View the conflicts and harms in your life as opportunities.
7. Listen deeply and compassionately to others, seeking to understand even if you don't agree with them. (Think about who you want to be in the latter situation rather than just being right.)
8. Engage in dialogue with others, even when what is being said is difficult, remaining open to learning from them and the encounter.
9. Be cautious about imposing your "truths" and views on other people and situations.
10. Sensitively confront everyday injustices including sexism, racism, and classism.

Reflection Strategies

There are many ways to engage in self-reflection. Individually, one may meditate or journal in response to questions like those outlined in the next section. One may use a structured process such as the one offered below. Community-based reflective practices might include joining support groups or holding affinity circles to explore questions or engaging with service or advocacy groups. We also encounter occasions for self-reflection on a daily basis when we take time to pause and be curious about our actions and interactions, asking ourselves questions about what went well or did not go well and why, what we could have done differently, or what else might be happening for the other person. Additional strategies for reflection can include mental health counseling, spiritual direction, and education to gain additional perspective and clarity on your or others' experiences. What is most important is that we continually reflect on how our current experiences may be interfacing with and influenced by past ones, so that our present actions and interactions can come from a restorative place, rather than a place of hurt.

Process for Personal Reflection

In preparation:

1. Find a comfortable, quiet place to sit. Gather a journal and writing implement, and any other materials that help you center yourself.
2. Before starting the exercise, ground yourself in abundant self-compassion and

acknowledge how you are feeling at this very moment.

3. Envision a place or person with whom you feel most safe. Pay attention to what you see, smell, hear, taste, or touch. If you wish, draw a sketch or find an object to hold that represents this image.

In reflection:

1. Select a topic from the ones outlined in the next section.
2. Reflect on the questions provided for that topic.

In closing:

1. Write out your reflections, especially any key lessons or insights that surfaced.
2. Consider if you need or desire to share what came up for you with someone else. This is not required; remember that no one is entitled to your story.
3. Take time to breathe, move, and send yourself abundant compassion.

As you feel moved, repeat this exercise with other topics and explore any common threads between them.

Reflection Questions

In this section, we offer reflection questions associated with the themes in this book. Responding to these questions will help you to develop a shorthand for responding restoratively in future circumstances. Before you begin to consider the questions, spend time preparing for reflection, as this is important for being fully present when you recall events and connect with yourself. Consider this reflection as an investment in your future restorative self.

Experiences with Community

Experiences with community can be good and bad, healthy and unhealthy, restorative and punitive. Recalling these experiences can help us identify restorative principles already present and areas in need of attention.

Reflection questions:

1. Think about groups that you belong to that do and do not have shared agreements about values and/or norms. When present, what are the agreements? How do group dynamics compare across those with and without agreements?
2. Reflect on the communities to which you belong. To what degree would you consider them "restorative"? What leads you to your conclusion? How could they be made more restorative?
3. Think about the communities that have had the greatest impact on you. What was/is the nature of that impact? What lessons can you gain from those experiences to create restorative communities?

Values

Values guide how we act and relate to one another. They can be a source of conflict when they are not aligned with others' or when a person's behaviors do not align with their stated values. Thus, it is important for each individual to name the values that they hold most dear. These personal values may mirror restorative values named earlier, or include others. Remember, values are aspirational; no one lives up to them perfectly 100 percent of the time. Still, identifying values helps us to bring our most authentic selves into relationship with others.

Reflection questions:

1. Name and write down three to five core values that inform how you desire to live in right relationship. When, in your life, are these values most present? When are they most challenging to live out?
2. What values are important for a strong community or for you to feel nourished by your communities?
3. What do you think are the most important values for a community to have? How can and do you live out these values in your daily community life or when supporting those that have caused harm or been harmed?

Barriers to Community

Earlier, we discussed barriers to community: interpersonal barriers, including struggling to listen, withholding empathy, and showing intolerance for difference; and structural barriers, especially white supremacy. It is important to be honest with ourselves (and, if necessary, with others) about our own participation in and experience with each of these barriers. Even the most well-intentioned community members may have blind spots when it comes to these barriers, especially the impact of white supremacy and racial harms among those people who benefit from it and other forms of privilege. Our reluctance and failure to examine these barriers in ourselves has the potential, at best, to stifle the opportunities for harm repair and community building and, at worst, to cause further harm to community members.

In order to address social justice issues that arise in the best possible ways, communities must observe the ways these barriers, especially white supremacy, challenge their progress and cause harm.

Ultimately, we need to explore our willingness to humanize others.

Reflection questions:

1. When are you a good listener and when do you find it difficult to listen well?
2. What draws you toward or causes you to shy away from listening to people who have been harmed or caused harm?
3. To what degree are you able to walk in the shoes of a person with whom you are diametrically opposed or do not relate to? What gets in the way of being empathetic? What can you do to be more aware of and empathetic of others' experiences?
4. Recall an instance when you offered your time and attention to a person who holds different values than you or may have been on the other side of a conflict. What was that experience like for you?
5. What is your own experience with collective and/or intergenerational trauma? To what degree has that trauma been healed or transformed?
6. How do you respond when someone wants to talk about experiences with white supremacy

and/or collective or intergenerational trauma? To what degree is your response restorative or harmful to individuals and community?

7. How may white supremacy be at work in your day-to-day life, interpersonal relationships, and your community?

Being Harmed and Causing Harm

We all have experience being harmed and causing harm. These experiences and their aftermath can shape how we respond to others' experience with being harmed and causing harm.

Reflection questions:

Think back on times when you (1) were harmed by an individual or community and then (2) caused harm to someone else. These experiences do not need to be crimes or even severe in nature, but they should be memories in which you can clearly locate yourself. If it is helpful, jot a few experiences down. Select one experience when you were the harmed party and then a different experience when you were the person who caused harm. Consider the following questions.

1. What happened?
2. What were you thinking about at the time and what did you need?
3. What happened in the aftermath of this incident? What was your response and/or that of others? For example, was it retributive, restorative, or both? Were you blamed, ambivalent, forthcoming, ignored, or dismissed?
4. How did your own or others' responses align with or violate values that are important to you?

5. Did you or others take any responsibility for what happened? What did accountability look like in this instance? Did it serve to repair the wrongs done? If not, what would a restorative response have looked like and how might it have changed the outcome?
6. What came about as a result of this event and responses? How were you affected? What feelings arose for you then or now?
7. What did you learn from this experience? How has it shaped your responses or reactions to being harmed and/or causing harm over time and your views of community?
8. If something like this were to happen again, to you or a loved one, what would you do differently?

Responding to Harm as a Community Member

The road to finding the best way to respond when we are needed requires reflection on questions that help us assess our own strengths and limitations in responding to harm in the community, especially as it relates to our own experiences of being harmed or causing harm.

Reflection questions:

1. In what ways, if any, have I judged people who have been harmed or caused harm? How can I avoid being judgmental when engaging with people impacted by or involved in harm?
2. What are my "hot button" issues? What is my self-care plan if an involved party to the harm has a similar issue?

3. Based on my reflections on being harmed and causing harm (above), what new insights or lessons do I have about responding to harm?

Building Restorative Communities

The twelve principles of restorative community represent the aspirational ways we can be fully present in our communities for one another. While they may not come easily to everyone, reflection may reveal new ways to be a good member of the community. We offer one set of questions for each principle.

Reflection questions:

1. In your community, what values have been named or assumed by the collective? When would be a natural moment to revisit shared values as a group?
2. When have you felt a sense of mutuality in communities? How can you cultivate that across your communities?
3. What gifts, talents, successes, and strengths are already present in your community and how can you, together with other community members, build upon these?
4. What norms, policies, or procedures are currently in effect in your community? To what degree were they created together? What would it look like to revisit and refine these together in light of restorative values, principles, and practices?
5. How do you extend welcome to newcomers? What can you do personally to improve? How can your community make plans to welcome others with intention?

6. Reflect on a time that your community needed to learn about something together. How did you go about doing that? What might have changed if there had been more opportunity to listen to others along the way?
7. What does celebration look like in your community? To what degree does it include relational ways of affirming one another or allowing time for rest?
8. To what degree do you know people in your communities? Even if you have known others in your community for a long time, what are ways you can (re)connect with them more deeply?
9. How have you responded when challenges arise in the life of the community? How can you take time to pause and consider the impacts, needs, and obligations of the group?
10. When decisions are made in your community, to what degree do members feel that they all have a chance to contribute? What is one upcoming decision where you could try using a consensus model?
11. In what ways can you allow conflict to become a more transcendent vehicle to get through a difficult circumstance? What would it take to engage conflict with curiosity or wonder, and not with anger?
12. What partners do you need to build the community you want to see and live in? Who can help carry the load when there are tough circumstances?

Roles and Responsibilities

Recall that there are a number of roles that a community member can play in a formal restorative process or in building toward restorative communities. In order to lend our support to the creation of restorative communities, it is important to reflect on our own gifts, talents, and capacities as well as account for our limitations and areas for growth. With this knowledge, we may seek out others who complement us and our contributions. Doing so also communicates an appreciation for what others bring to the table.

Reflection Questions:

1. What roles have you played in your various communities—work, family, civic organizations, or social groups? Were those roles assigned or volunteered? How did you feel when taking on that role?
2. Recall a time when you felt like you were thriving in your role. What contributed to that feeling? Where did you sense comfort, confidence, or hear affirmation from others?
3. Recall a time that you struggled in a role. What made it uncomfortable or difficult? How did you experience messages of critique (from yourself or others)? What did you learn about yourself through that experience?
4. Think about the restorative community that you desire to be part of. Who do you need to join you in creating that community because of the roles and gifts they offer? How can you strengthen your relationship with that person(s)?

5. What role(s) do you feel drawn to that are necessary to build a restorative community? What draws you to that role? Does it come to you naturally, have you received training in the necessary skills, or is it an area about which you desire to learn or grow?

Conclusion

You don't need to answer all these questions at once. You are encouraged to come back to them individually or as groups, when needs and opportunities arise. When individuals continually take a look at themselves, their reflective stance enables them to speak and act from a place of authenticity, humility, and intentionality. Building restorative communities requires this constant attention to doing the work to remain in right relationship with one another. Like gardening, being in good community requires regular work, nurturing, and a mindful presence. All of these actions lead us toward the existence of what promises to be a beloved community, as we will discover in the next chapter.

Chapter 9
Realizing Beloved Community

We can create the Beloved Community. It's not an utopia, but is realistic and achievable, a society of justice and love. It's not conflict-free, but shuns acquiescence to violence.

—Dr. Bernice A. King[1]

There is a form of Japanese art called *kintsugi*, in which pieces of broken pottery are put back together using gold. The repaired vessel is made whole again in a way that makes its former areas of separation more visible, but also more beautiful and more valuable because of its brokenness. This image is useful for understanding restorative responses to harm and restorative communities. Rather than thinking that we need to throw the pieces away or create or maintain a "perfect vessel," we slow down, consider the realities of the rupture and the broken and bruised parts of relationships in need of mending, and inquire about needs for repair and how we, in community, can contribute. The answers that emerge over time will be the gold that fuses the clay of trust and connection. The community "vessel," that restorative community, is now more beautiful and valuable, if not beloved, than it was before.

Similarly, restorative justice approaches and restorative communities are paths toward MLK's vision for the beloved community, described in Chapter 1. The underpinnings of these paths are:

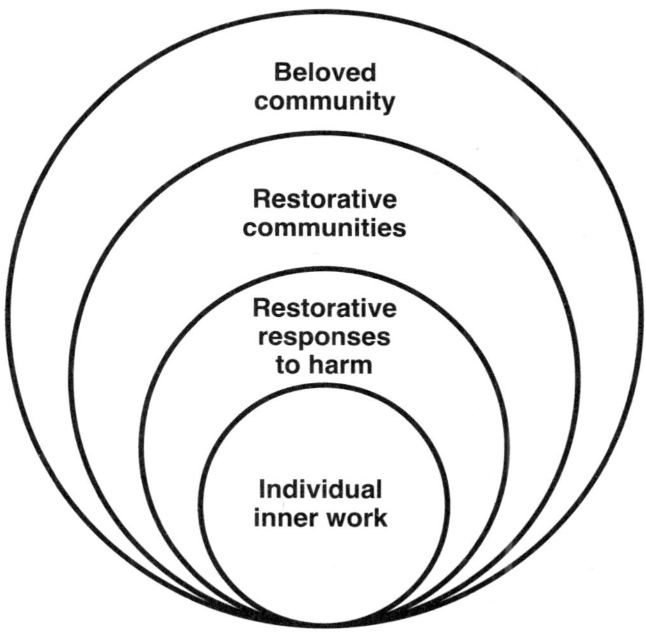

- A restorative self, achieved by developing self-awareness that helps us to gravitate toward the right roles in community;
- Restorative approaches to interpersonal harm, understanding what restorative justice is, and, when harm occurs, identifying how

to respond as a community member who might not be directly impacted by the harm;
- Restorative communities, realized by practicing restorative community principles and taking on authentic roles.

These three underpinnings have the power to be incubators for resilience, empathy, healing, belonging, and accountability. They have the potential to shape the hearts and minds of individuals, who then bring these mindsets into other environments and groups. Furthermore, individuals and communities may model to others what is possible when we prioritize right relationship. The ripple effects of this kind of presence have the potential to shift the very ground beneath our collective feet and bring forth a world that is more whole, more beloved than before.

This invitation to restorative justice, restorative community, and beloved community may feel like we are discussing the existence of unicorns, leprechauns, or any other elusive figures in history. It may seem countercultural, as it asks us to choose healing over punishment, dialogue over adversariness, and human connection over procedures and protocols. Interconnectedness in community can be both complex and beautiful. Forging ubuntu is multi-faceted and can be daunting. Just because "I am" does not always mean "we are." Yet, with individual commitments to restorative justice philosophy and practice, principles of restorative community, and inner work, it is achievable. In a sense, creating restorative and beloved communities is a pattern of "wash, rinse, repeat," where the commitment is regularly renewed.

The world in which we proposed this book is different from the world in which it is published—and perhaps even more different still from the time in which you are reading it. At this moment, a beloved community feels elusive and as though it is shifting daily. That said, relationships are always relevant, and it will always be necessary to use what we have proposed.

This was also true for us as authors. Many times, our best-laid plans for writing were set aside when a community crisis arose in need of our attention, professionally or personally. There were also ways in which we were spurred on to consider not only the content of our writing, but also the connection, resilience, and hope that we found in our relationships with one another as coauthors.

When we began this book, both of us shared stories about when we did not know how to respond in a community situation as good neighbors. Given the lessons of this book, we each came to new reflections on our own roles and contributions as neighbors.

When my neighbor's son was killed, I attended a vigil and contributed to a pot of funds to cover funeral and other expenses. I also instilled a sense of community in my children. When my oldest son asked me what jails look like, I described what I saw in my visits with people who were incarcerated. I told him that while the people I met had done bad things, they were not bad people and that many were working to make changes in their lives, that they were wise and caring, and that I was

> lucky to call some of them my friends. He then asked if, when they come out of jail, they are our neighbors. My mama heart melted. My son had a conception of "neighbor" that went beyond those who lived on our street. Honoring his question and my deepest convictions, I said: "Yes, my darling, people in jail are our neighbors."
>
> —Caitlin

> During a trip to Chicago, I convened members of the local restorative justice community. The venue was stunning—comfortable, welcoming, with beautiful art on the walls—which made greeting our guests feel effortless. Some were new connections, others felt like old friends.
>
> When the doors opened to the dining area, we found an abundance of savory and sweet delights. As nearly forty people gathered, our hostess shared the history of the space, and we gave thanks for the meal. I sensed some were waiting for "the agenda" or perhaps a fundraising pitch. To ease their minds, I paused and said that there was no agenda, and no ask. Our only intention was to be together, to let them know they were seen, and to lift them a little higher than when they arrived.
>
> For me, that gathering was a glimpse of the beloved community I long to see.
>
> —Sheryl

As you move on, remember that you are always a member of the community! Being a good community member is not a role to put on and take off. Live as a restorative community member and you will always be prepared to respond to harm and conflict. Build restorative communities wherever you are, and together we may crescendo toward the vision of beloved community.

> And God has put you here to make this earth more like a beloved community like the kingdom of Heaven. And you are the angels of earth. Go forth and never forget who you are and where you came from and how many people sacrificed and suffered to make it possible for you to be all that you are, and all that you're going to be.
>
> —Andrew Young, prominent figure in the Civil Rights Movement and former Ambassador to the United Nations[2]

Recommended Resources

Barriers to Community

- Fania Davis. *The Little Book of Race and Restorative Justice: Black Lives, Healing, and US Social Transformation*. Good Books, 2019.
- Bessel van der Kolk and Sean Pratt. *The Body Keeps the Score.* Penguin Random House Audio Publishing Group, 2021.
- Remaa Menakem. *My Grandmother's Hands: Racialized Trauma and the Pathway to Mending Our Hearts and Bodies*. Penguin Books, 2021.
- Edward Valandra and Robert Yazzie. *Colorizing Restorative Justice: Voicing Our Realities*. Living Justice Press, 2020.
- Carolyn Yoder. *The Little Book of Trauma Healing: When Violence Strikes and Community Security Is Threatened*. Good Books, 2020.

Restorative Justice

- Howard Zehr. *Big Book of Restorative Justice*. Good Books, 2015.
- Howard Zehr. *Changing Lenses: Restorative Justice for Our Times*. Herald Press, 2015.

Restorative Community

- Amy Potter Czajkowsk and David Anderson Hooker. *Transforming Historical Harms.* Coming to the Table, 2013.
- Kay Pranis, Barry Stuart, and Mark Wedge. *Peacemaking Circles: From Conflict to Community.* Living Justice Press, 2003.

Roles, Responsibilities, and Restorative Self

- Alisa Del Tufo and E. Quin Gonell. *The Little Book of Restorative Justice Program Design: Using Participatory Action Research to Build and Assess RJ Initiatives.* Good Books, 2023.
- Shawn Ginwright. *The Four Pivots: Reimagining Justice, Reimagining Ourselves.* Huichin, unceded Ohlone land, a.k.a. Berkeley, CA: North Atlantic Books, 2022.

Endnotes

Chapter 1

1 Martin Luther King, "Advice for Living, November 1957," The Martin Luther King, Jr. Research and Education Institute, *Ebony Magazine*, https://kinginstitute.stanford.edu/king-papers/documents/advice-living-1, 106.

2 "The King Philosophy—Nonviolence365®," The King Center, December 5, 2022, https://thekingcenter.org/about-tkc/the-king-philosophy/.

3 "The question: What does ubuntu really mean?" *The Guardian*, September 28, 2006.

4 Desmond Tutu, "Who we are: Human uniqueness and the African spirit of Ubuntu," posted April 3, 2013 by Templeton Prize, YouTube, https://www.youtube.com/watch?v=0wZtfqZ271w.

Chapter 2

1 "Teaching and Learning," National Museum of African American History & Culture, Smithsonian Institute, https://nmaahc.si.edu/learn/talking-about-race/topics/community-building.

Chapter 3

1 bell hooks, *Killing Rage* (Henry Holt and Company, 1995), 35.

2 Brené Brown, *Daring Greatly: How the Courage to Be Vulnerable Transforms the Way We Live, Love, Parent, and Lead* (Avery, 2015).

3 Perry, T. (2021, April 25). Speech presented at the 93rd Academy Awards. Retrieved from https://aaspeechesdb.oscars.org/link/093-25/.
4 "Doctrine of Discovery," Upstander Project, https://upstanderproject.org/learn/guides-and-resources/first-light/doctrine-of-discovery.
5 Carolyn Yoder, *The Little Book of Trauma Healing: When Violence Strikes and Community Security Is Threatened* (Good Books, 2005).

Chapter 4

1 Davis, F. E. (2012). What's love got to do with it? *Tikkun, 27*(1), 30–33. https://www.tikkun.org/whats-love-got-to-do-with-it/.
2 Howard Zehr, *The Little Book of Restorative Justice: Revised and Updated* (Good Books, 2015), 51.
3 "The Navajo Response to Crime," *Justice as Healing* Vol. 3, no.2 (Summer 1998).
4 "The Slow Leadership Framework: A Humanizing, Social Justice Approach to Leadership," OSCLG: Social Justice Strategy, 2025.
5 "Truth and Reconciliation Commission, South Africa," *Encyclopedia Britannica*, https://www.britannica.com/topic/Truth-and-Reconciliation-Commission-South-Africa.
6 "The Commission in Maine," Upstander Project, https://upstanderproject.org/learn/guides-and-resources/first-light/truth-and-reconciliation-commission.

Chapter 5

1 Howard Zehr, "On Safe Spaces," July 22, 2016, https://emu.edu/now/restorative-justice/2016/07/22/on-safe-spaces/.

Chapter 6

1 Henri Nouwen, "Community Makes God Visible," Henri Nouwen Society, November 26, 2024, https://henrinouwen.org/meditations/community-makes-god-visible/.
2 "Resilience," American Psychological Association, https://www.apa.org/topics/resilience.

3 Community Restorative Justice Hubs, https://rjhubs.org/.

Chapter 7

1 Coretta Scott King, "King's Widow Urges Acts of Compassion," *Los Angeles Times*, January 17, 2000, https://www.latimes.com/archives/la-xpm-2000-jan-17-mn-54832-story.html.

2 Ericka Sasson et al., "Because We Need Each Other, Part I: Origin Story," *Convergence*, April 2, 2025, https://convergencemag.com/articles/we-care-for-each-other-we-fight-for-each-other-mutual-aid-and-power-building/.

Chapter 8

1 Richard Rohr, "Transforming Pain—a Daily Meditation by Fr. Richard Rohr," Center for Action and Contemplation, October 18, 2018, https://cac.org/daily-meditations/transforming-pain-2018-10-17/.

2 Howard Zehr. *Big Book of Restorative Justice*. Good Books, 2015.

Chapter 9

1 "Who We Are," The King Center, August 17, 2021, https://thekingcenter.org/about-tkc/.

2 Operation HOPE, Inc. (2024, December 19). *Closing remarks: Ambassador Andrew Young at HOPE Global Forums 2024 [Video]*. https://www.facebook.com/share/v/1BAT2STPJv/.